Building Safe Driving Skills
THIRD EDITION

Building Safe Driving Skills

THIRD EDITION

Patrick Kelley
Instructor of Driver Education
Hayward Unified School District
Hayward, California

Consultants:

Neal H. Rathjen
Curriculum Specialist
Driver Education and Safety
Milwaukee Public Schools
Milwaukee, Wisconsin

William J. Harris
Supervisor of Safety and Driver Education
Board of Administration Building
Dade County Public Schools
Miami, Florida

Fred English
Supervisor of Driver Education
Los Angeles Unified School District
Los Angeles, California

GLENCOE
Macmillan/McGraw-Hill

Lake Forest, Illinois   Columbus, Ohio   Mission Hills, California   Peoria, Illinois

Send all inquiries to:
GLENCOE DIVISION
Macmillan/McGraw-Hill
15319 Chatsworth Street
P.O. Box 9609
Mission Hills, CA 91346-9609

Diagrams and charts by Russ Keever.

Chapter opening illustrations and other art by Dick Cole.

Road map and map legend, pages 210 and 211, used by permission of The H. M. Gousha Company.

Copyright © 1986 by Glencoe Publishing Company, a division of Macmillan, Inc.

All rights reserved. No part of this book shall be reproduced or transmitted in any form or by any means, electronic or mechanical, including photocopying, recording, or by any information or retrieval system, without written permission from the Publisher.

Library of Congress Catalog Card Number: 85-81742

Printed in the United States of America
ISBN 0-02-831570-7 (Student Text)
ISBN 0-02-831600-2 (Teacher's Guide)
ISBN 0-02-831580-4 (Student Workbook)
ISBN 0-02-831590-1 (Chapter Tests)

2 3 4 5 6 7 8 9   95 94 93 92 91

Contents

	Preface	7
1	Are You Ready, Willing, and Able?	8
2	Your Personality, and How It Affects Your Driving	26
3	Nature's Traffic Laws and Car Control	38
4	Traffic Laws and You	54
5	What Are Your Driver Responsibilities?	76
6	How a Car Works	86
7	Inside the Car	100
8	Now It's Your Turn To Take the Wheel	114
9	Turning, Backing, and Parking	126
10	Driving in Traffic	144
11	The Pedestrian	156
12	Highways and Freeways	168
13	Motorcycles	186
14	Ready for Anything	194
15	Planning a Trip	208
16	Owning a Car	216
	Index	235

Preface

So you want to drive a car. You are old enough now, and you are ready to learn. You may feel ready to get behind the wheel right now. But there is a lot more to driving than just knowing how to operate an automobile.

Just because a person *wants* a driver's license does not mean he or she will get one. A state does not *owe* anyone a driver's license. A person must *earn* his or her license.

The laws for getting a driver's license are not the same in every state. But they agree on most important things. Before a person can get a driver's license, the person must show that he or she:

- can drive a car safely.

- knows the traffic laws.

- knows all the traffic signs and signals.

- knows the state laws about insurance, accidents, and other things having to do with driving.

The easiest part of learning to drive is learning how to make the car go. But there is much to learn before you get behing the wheel. *Building Safe Driving Skills* will help you to learn what you must know. It will help you to learn to drive a car. But more important, it will help you to drive *well* and drive *safely*.

CHAPTER **1**

Are You Ready, Willing, and Able?

It was a warm spring morning in 1905. Frank Mills was getting ready to visit his brother in Greentown. The last time Frank had visited his brother he had used his horse and wagon. But this trip was going to be different. Frank was going to drive to Greentown in his new automobile.

Frank's neighbors were there to see him off. This was the first automobile many of them had ever seen up close. "How fast will she go, Mr. Mills?" asked one boy. "Well," Frank answered, "they tell me she can go up to 25 miles an hour. But I have never had her up to more than 15 miles an hour."

"15 miles an hour! That means you could get to Greentown in just two hours!"

"I *could*, if the road was flat and dry all the way," said Frank. "But it would be very dangerous to drive that fast."

"You would never get *me* into one of those things," the boy's father said. "I'll take a horse and wagon *any* day."

Frank smiled. "Wait and see. In a few years, you will all be driving automobiles."

It took quite a while to get the car started. But at last, with a bang and a puff of smoke, the engine began running. Frank jumped into the car and rolled off down the road.

At first, all went well. In an hour, Frank had gone almost ten miles. But then it began to rain. Frank had a hard time keeping the car on the wet road. More and more rain fell. The road became a sea of mud. Frank kept on trying. But the car did not have enough power to go on. It came to a stop, all four wheels deep in the soft mud.

Frank jumped out and walked to a farm down the road. "Can you help me get my car out of the mud?" he asked the farmer. "Sure," the farmer said. "I'll get my horse and we will pull you out. These roads are not made for automobiles."

It was night by the time Frank got to Greentown. The 30-mile trip had taken 12 hours. Frank was cold and wet and covered with mud. "What do you think of your automobile now?" his brother asked him. "One day things will be different," Frank answered. "Wait and see. Things will change."

Driving for Today and Tomorrow

Frank Mills was right. Things have changed a lot since 1905. Roads have changed, and so have automobiles. Roads are much better today than they were back then. And there are a lot more roads, too. In 1905, there were only about 160,000 miles of paved roads in the United States. Today, there are almost two million miles of paved roads.

There are also a lot more cars. In 1905, there were 78,800 automobiles on the road. Today, there are more than 320 million cars. And the cars are a lot different from those of 1905. Frank Mills' car could only go 25 miles an hour. Now, cars can easily go 55 miles an hour or more.

It took Frank Mills 12 hours to drive 30 miles. A driver on a freeway today can drive 30 miles in 33 minutes at 55 miles an hour. In one day he can drive hundreds of miles. He does not have to be afraid of getting caught in the mud, or getting cold and wet if it rains.

In many ways, driving today is much easier than it was in 1905. But in other ways, driving is a lot harder. Every year, over 45,000 people are killed in traffic accidents. 3⅕ *million* people are hurt.

Why are there so many accidents? New roads are safer than ever. And cars today have many safety features that older cars did not have. But still the number of accidents keeps going up. Why? The answer is not hard to find. *Most accidents happen because of bad driving.*

What can be done to cut down on the number of accidents? Again, the answer is not hard to find. If people were better drivers, there would not be so many accidents. This is where Driver Education can help. Driver Education *can* and *does* help people to drive better. Those who have had Driver Education have fewer accidents than those who have not.

What makes these people better drivers? Again, there is an easy answer. Because of Driver Education, these drivers *know more*. They know more about driving. They know more about the rules of the road. And most important of all, they know more about *themselves*.

Each year thousands of new drivers get behind the wheel for the first time. This year, you will be one of these drivers. What you will learn in this class will help you to become a good driver. There is a lot to learn. Knowing how to start, stop, and steer a car is only one part of it. To become a good driver, the first thing you must learn about is *yourself*.

Physical Condition

You would not want to drive a car like the one shown here. A good driver would never think of driving such a car. The physical condition of the car is quite bad. It has only one headlight, and no tail lights. The windshield is broken. And the tires are worn. Because of its poor physical condition, this car is not safe to drive.

A good driver always checks the physical condition of the car he is driving. He checks the lights, the horn, the brakes, and the condition of the tires. Only if everything is working right will he start driving. He knows that a car in poor physical condition can not be driven safely.

The physical condition of the driver is just as important. A driver in poor physical condition may not be able to drive safely. Sometimes, because of his physical condition, a person can not get a driv-

er's license. The Department of Motor Vehicles will not issue him a driver's license. A blind person, for example, could never get a driver's license. To be a good driver, a person should be able to see well.

Many people have some physical problem or other. But, often, a person with a physical problem can still become a good driver. If he does not see well, for example, he can go to an eye doctor. The doctor may have the person get glasses to help him see better. By wearing glasses, the person may be able to see well enough to drive safely.

How Well Can You See?

Before you start driving, you should have your eyes tested. Being able to see well is very important. You may have an eye problem you do not know about. An eye doctor can test your eyes. He will tell you if you have any problems. It is best to find out about problems *before* you get behind the wheel.

Many eye problems can be corrected. Many drivers correct their eye problems by wearing glasses.

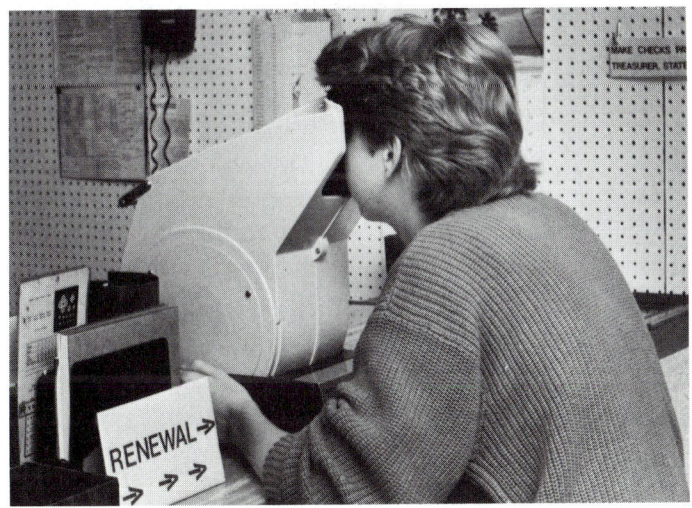

Every person who goes for a driver's license must take an eye test. The test shows if the person can see well enough to drive safely.

Other eye problems can not be corrected. But persons with these problems can still become good drivers. Because they know about their problems, they drive with more care.

To drive safely, a person must be able to see clearly. He must be able to see things that are close to him. And he must be able to see things that are far away. How clearly can you see? Here is a test you can take to find out.

> D C E P F
> R N Y Z O

Have a classmate hold this chart in good light. Stand about 15 feet away and cover one eye with a card. Walk slowly toward the chart. Try to read the letters out loud. When you can read seven or more of the letters, stop walking. How far are you from the chart? If you are 10 feet from the chart, the eye tested is normal. If you are 12 feet away, the eye is better than normal. If you are 8 feet away, the eye is below normal. Now take the test again. Cover your other eye and try reading the letters. Are your eyes normal, better than normal, or below normal?

Seeing to the Sides

There is more to seeing well than just seeing clearly. To drive safely, you must be able to see things in front of you. But you must be able to see things on both sides, too. When you drive, you must be able to see things "out of the corner of your eye." Here is another test you can take in class. It will help you find out how far to each side you can see things.

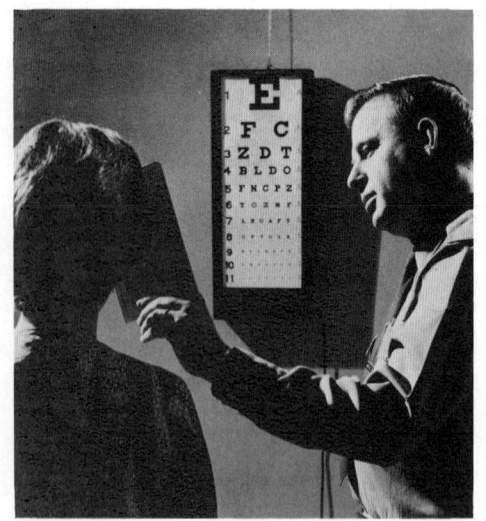

Make a card like the one shown here. Hold the card up to your nose. Look straight ahead. Now, have a classmate move a pencil slowly along the outside of the card. Have the person move the pencil from the back to the front. *Keep looking straight ahead.* As soon as you can see the moving pencil, tell your classmate to stop.

Now take the test again. This time have your classmate move the pencil along the other side of the card. Take the test five or six times on each side. At what point along the card can you first see the moving pencil? Most people can see the pencil before it gets to Point *A*. To drive safely, you should be able to see the pencil before it gets to Point *B*.

A person who can not see the pencil until after Point *B* has a problem. He can not see out of the corner of his eye. But such a person can still become a good driver. If he knows about his problem, he can do something about it. When he drives, he must look around more than other drivers. He must keep looking to the left and right. Because of his eye problem, he must drive with more care.

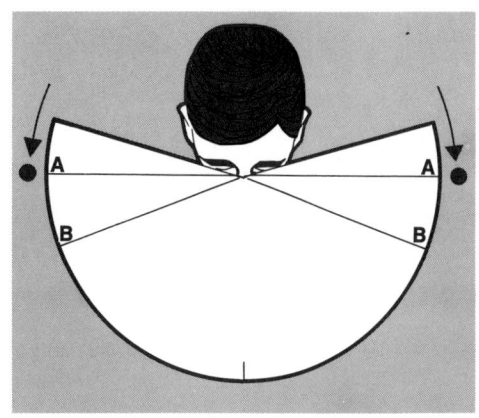

Seeing at Night

Some people can not see well at night. They can see fine as long as the sun is up. But after dark, they have a hard time seeing things. A person who can not see well at night has a driving problem. But as long as he knows about the problem, he can still drive safely. He knows that he should not drive at night. But if he has to drive at night, he drives with great care.

Even if your eyes are normal, you must be very careful when driving at night. Driving at night is much more dangerous than driving in daytime. Always drive more slowly at night. Before you get behind the wheel, make sure your windshield and headlights are clean. Watch out for pedestrians crossing the road. Be ready for anything.

The headlights of another car may blind you. For a short time, you may not be able to see what is ahead. Some people take longer than others to get over being blinded by another car's headlights. When you drive at night, try to keep from getting blinded. And try to keep from blinding other drivers.

If you are driving on a dark road, you may have your high-beam headlights on. When you see another car coming toward you, lower your headlights. The driver of the other car should lower his, too. But his headlights can still blind you. To keep this from happening, do not look straight at them. Slow down. Keep watching the road ahead, but look a little to the right. Look straight ahead again only after the other car has passed.

How well you see at night depends on your physical condition. On some nights you may not see as well. Or it may take longer to get over being blinded by someone's high beams.

How Far and How Fast?

Your eyes do more than just tell you what is ahead on the road. Suppose you are driving along on the road shown here. You have slowed down to make a left turn. You can see that another car is coming toward you. Is it safe to turn? Or should you wait for the car to go by? What things must you judge to know if it is safe to turn?

You must be able to judge how far away the other car is. And you must also be able to judge how fast it is coming toward you. Many new drivers have a hard time judging these things. As time goes by, most new drivers get better at it. But some do not. Some drivers are never quite sure how far away another car is. They are not sure how fast it is moving.

A person who has this problem must be more careful. When following another car, he leaves plenty of space between his car and the car ahead. He makes sure he has more than enough time to pass another car safely. When making a left turn, he also gives himself more than enough time and space. If he is not sure he can turn safely, he waits until he *is* sure. This is a good rule for all drivers. Don't take chances.

Seeing Colors

Being able to see colors well is important in driving. The colors of a traffic signal, for example, tell the driver what to do. A red light means stop. A yellow light means slow. And a green light means go.

Many people can not see colors well. Some can not tell red from green. People who can not see colors well are color blind. But a color blind person can still learn to drive safely. He may not be able to tell red from green. But he learns that the red light in a traffic signal is at the top. The yellow light is in the middle. And the green light is at the bottom.

How Well Can You Hear?

Seeing well is only one part of being in good physical condition. A driver should also be able to hear well. He should be able to hear the horn signals of other cars. There are many other important sounds

18

he should also be able to hear. The pictures on this page show some of the things a driver should be able to hear. What other things can you think of?

A driver who can not hear well must look around more. His eyes must do more work. What he can not hear, he must try to see. He must be ready for danger ahead, behind, and on both sides.

How Well Do You Feel?

Most of us are in good health most of the time. But just about everybody gets sick now and then. Few people can say they have never had a cold or an upset stomach. A driver who is not feeling well may not be able to drive safely. He may have a hard time keeping his mind on what he is doing. He may not be able to see or think as clearly.

A good driver knows he should not drive when he is not feeling well. If he must drive, he drives with great care. He tries to keep his mind on his driving. He does not drive as fast.

A person does not have to be sick to not feel well. He may feel bad because he is worried about something. A person who is worried or upset may not be able to drive safely. His mind is on other things. He does not watch the road with enough care.

Being sick or upset can change the way a person feels. So can being tired or sleepy. When a driver is tired, he does not see as clearly. And he is not as quick. There may be a stop sign ahead which he does not see at first. He may not see it in time to stop. The picture here shows what can happen.

Do not drive when you feel sleepy. If you become sleepy when you are driving, pull over and stop. Get some sleep if you can. You will feel better when you get up.

You may not always be able to stop at a place where you can sleep. But you can still get out of the car and take a short walk. Or you might stop somewhere for a cup of coffee. Even washing your face with cold water will help. When you begin driving again, keep a window open. Be sure there is lots of fresh air in the car.

Carbon Monoxide

Breathing carbon monoxide can also make you sleepy. This is another reason for making sure you have lots of fresh air. Carbon monoxide is a gas that is part of your car's exhaust. You can not see it, taste it, or smell it. Sometimes, carbon monoxide gets inside a car because of a leak in the exhaust system. Breathing it can make you sleepy and give you a headache. If you breathe enough carbon monoxide, it will kill you.

A worn out exhaust system is dangerous. Carbon monoxide can leak into the car if the exhaust system has a hole in it.

Breathing even a little carbon monoxide is dangerous. Because you can not smell it, you may not know you are breathing it. But the more you breathe, the more the gas slows down your thinking. In a short time, you may not know what you are doing. You may cause an accident.

Here are some things you can do about the dangers of carbon monoxide.

- Be sure the exhaust system does not leak.
- Keep the vents or windows open a little so you will have fresh air, even in the winter.
- Never run the engine in a closed garage. All cars put out carbon monoxide, even new ones with emission controls.
- Keep the engine in good running condition. An engine that is not running well puts out more carbon monoxide in its exhaust.

Alcohol and Drugs

The person who drinks and then drives is a danger to himself and others. Behind the wheel of a car, the drinking driver too often becomes a killer. In every 100 accidents in which someone was killed, 50 of the drivers had been drinking.

Alcohol changes a person's physical condition. The more alcohol a person drinks, the more it changes him. *But the change starts with the first drink.* The person does not see or hear as well. He can not move as quickly. He may even have a hard time walking straight.

Alcohol also changes the way a person feels and thinks. After a few drinks, a person may begin to do foolish things. But to him, these things do not seem foolish at all. He is no longer thinking clearly.

The most foolish thing he can do is get behind the wheel and drive. He still thinks that he can drive well. He may even feel that drinking makes him drive *better*. This is not so. Even one drink makes a person less able to drive safely. The number of accidents caused by drivers who had been drinking shows this. A person should never drink and then drive.

Drugs can also change a person's physical condition. They can change the way he feels and thinks. Most drugs are made to be used as medicines. Used with care, drugs can be of great help. But drugs can also be dangerous. A person should take drugs only if his doctor tells him to.

Even then he must be careful. Some drugs can make a person sleepy. Other drugs can change the way a person sees things. Like alcohol, drugs can change a person without his knowing it. He may still feel all right. But he may no longer be able to drive safely.

Ask your doctor about any pills or other drugs he may have you take. Find out if it is safe to drive after taking the pills. Even cold pills and headache pills can make it dangerous for you to drive.

Fit To Drive

You have seen that a person's physical condition has a lot to do with his driving. Many people have some physical problem or other. But most people with physical problems can still become good drivers. As long as a person knows about his problem, he can do something about it.

The good driver knows that his physical condition may change. There are times when even the best driver may not be able to drive safely. For example, a person may get sleepy while driving. Because he is tired, he does not see things as clearly. He is not as quick. The good driver watches for changes in his physical condition. He knows that if he is to drive safely, he must feel fit. He must feel fit when he starts driving. He must feel fit every minute he is behind the wheel.

Checking What You Have Read

1. Some people can not see things clearly that are far away. This is one kind of eye problem. List three other kinds of eye problems.
2. Suppose a person can not see very well "out of the corner of his eye." What can this person do to make up for his problem when he drives?
3. Which is more dangerous, driving in the day or driving at night?
4. What can you do to keep from being blinded by the headlights of another car?
5. Suppose a person is not very good at judging how far away things are. What can he do about this problem when he drives?
6. What does "color blind" mean?
7. What can a driver who is color blind do to make up for his problem?
8. List three kinds of things a person should listen for when driving.
9. What can a person who is hard of hearing do to make up for his problem?
10. Why might it be dangerous for a person to drive when he is worried or upset?
11. Suppose a person gets sleepy while he is driving. What is the *best* thing for him to do about it? Is there anything else he can do?
12. What is carbon monoxide? Why is it dangerous?

13. List four things a driver can do to cut down the danger of carbon monoxide.
14. How does alcohol change a person's physical condition?
15. How does alcohol change the way a person feels and thinks?
16. How do drugs change physical condition?
17. Is a person's physical condition always the same? List six things that can change it.

To Talk About

1. Can a person with a physical problem become a good driver? Can he become even better than some drivers that do not have physical problems? Why or why not?
2. Taking drugs "for the fun of it" is foolish. But taking drugs and then driving is even more foolish. Why?
3. Every year thousands of people are killed because of drivers who drink and then drive. What can be done to keep drinking drivers off the road? Are new laws needed? What would you do about this problem? What kind of laws would you make?

Things To Do

How have cars changed over the years? What safety features do new cars have? How do these safety features make driving easier and safer? Are still more safety features needed? Make a bulletin board display called "Automobiles — Then and Now." On one side of the bulletin board, show pictures of old cars. Cut the pictures from magazines or draw your own. On the other side of the bulletin board, show pictures of new cars. In what ways are the old cars and the new cars the same? In what ways have they changed? Also show pictures of what you think cars will look like in years to come. Draw your own.

CHAPTER 2

Your Personality, and How It Affects Your Driving

Bob Lupe sat in his car waiting for the light to change. Next to him was a girl he had met at school, Rita Landers. This was the first time Rita had ever been in Bob's car. She had already made up her mind it would be the last time, too. The traffic signal changed to green and Bob pushed the accelerator to the floor. The car was off like an arrow, rear tires smoking. "Go, baby, go!" Bob said to his car. "Show Rita what you can do."

There was another car ahead and Bob had to slow down. But he did not slow down until he was almost on top of the other car. Then he hit the brakes hard. The other car was moving along just under the speed limit. Bob wanted to pass. But there was a lot of traffic coming the other way, and he could not. He blew his horn at the other driver. "Get moving or get off the road!" Bob roared.

Bob was right behind the car ahead. He blew his horn again and moved even closer. "What are you doing?"

said Rita. "Don't you know that tailgating is dangerous? Do you want to get into an accident?"

"This is the only way to get these old turtles moving," Bob answered. "And besides, tailgating is only dangerous if you don't know what you are doing."

The two cars were coming to a hill. Bob could not see over the hill. But he still pulled into the other lane and started to pass.

"Look out!" cried Rita. A bus was coming over the hill right at them. Bob passed the other car and got back in his own lane just in time.

"Are you trying to kill us?" Rita said.

"Don't worry," Bob answered. "I'm a good driver. I have never had an accident."

"Never?" the girl asked. "Then why is the front of your car all banged up the way it is?"

"Oh, that," Bob said. "That does not count. It was not my fault. I was crossing an intersection when this other car hit me. *He* was the one that caused the accident, not me. But he got what was coming to him. You should have seen the side of his car!"

"*What!*" said Rita. "You say he ran into you? With the *side* of his car? How could he do that?

"That is what the police asked, too," Bob said. "But what do they know about driving?"

Driving Personality

With all of Bob's wild driving, he did not have an accident that day. Rita got home without being hurt. But she was upset. She liked Bob and wanted to see him again. She had thought she knew Bob pretty well. Now she wondered about it. He was one person when he was at school. But he seemed to become a different person when he got behind the wheel. Just like the story of Dr. Jekyll and Mr. Hyde. Rita began to think that she did not know the real Bob at all.

Just about all of us have met someone like Bob. When not driving, the person is as nice as can be. But once behind the wheel, the person seems to change. He has one personality when not driving. But he has another personality as well. This is his driving personality.

A person's driving personality can make him a good driver or a bad driver. It has little to do with how well he can operate an automobile. Take Bob, for example. He knew a lot about cars. He had no physical problems that would keep him from becoming a good driver. Bob could have become a good driver if he had wanted to. (He thought he was!) But he had a poor driving personality. And because of his poor driving personality, he was a danger to himself and others.

There are many kinds of poor driving personalities. Not all bad drivers are like Bob. A person does not have to be a wild driver to be a bad driver. Let's take a look at some of the different kinds of poor driving personalities.

The Show-off

First, there is the person who likes to show off. He does things that he knows are foolish. But he wants to look like a big man. He drives his car as though it were a racing car. And he hopes people will think he looks like a big-time race driver. But few people, if any, do.

A race driver drives fast only in a race. Even then, he tries to drive as safely as he can. He does not take any chances that he does not have to take. The race driver knows how dangerous speed can be. The show-off may know this, too. But he does not seem to care. All he cares about is looking like a big man.

The Hot Head

The hot head does not smile much when he is driving. He does not smile because he is almost always angry about something. This kind of driver gets angry very quickly and for very little reason. As he sees it, everyone and everything is trying to get in his way. He gets angry if he has to wait for a long traffic signal. He blows his horn at other drivers ahead of him. He shouts at pedestrians trying to cross the street.

When a person is angry, he can not judge things as clearly. He does things he would not do at other times. He may pass another car on a hill or a curve. Because he is angry, he does not think about the danger.

The Nervous Driver

At first, the nervous driver may not seem like such a bad driver. He watches out for everything. He does not often drive fast. And he knows that driving can be dangerous. But the nervous driver is still a bad driver. He can cause accidents because of the way he drives.

The nervous driver is not sure of his driving skills. For him, driving is never much fun. He is always afraid that something bad will happen. He worries too much. Often, he drives too slow to keep up with traffic. He thinks that this is a good way to stay out of trouble. But driving too slow can be just as dangerous as driving too fast. Under most conditions, it is best to keep up with traffic.

The nervous driver gets excited easily. In heavy traffic, things often seem to be happening too fast for him. Sometimes he does not know what to do next. Because he is not sure of his driving, he may do the wrong thing.

One slow moving car can hold up a long line of traffic. A good driver keeps up with traffic or helps others to pass.

The Thoughtless Driver

Once the thoughtless driver gets in his car, he is in another world. The car is his own little world. People and things outside do not seem to be a part of this world. The thoughtless driver acts as though nothing else were real. If he backs into a parked car, he acts as if nothing had happened. He just drives away.

The thoughtless driver never thinks about others. He turns without making a signal. He pulls out into traffic when it is not safe to do so. Other drivers must slow down to keep from hitting him. At night, he keeps his high-beam headlights on even when another car is coming. He does not care that he is blinding the other driver. He would not like it if someone did this to him. But he does not care what he does to someone else.

The Road Hog

This is the kind of driver who thinks he owns the road. The road hog wants it all for himself. He may drive in such a way that other cars can not pass. He may drive down the middle of the road. Or he may speed up when another car starts to pass.

The road hog wants everyone to get out of his way. He pushes his way into traffic. When he passes, he comes very close to the car ahead. Going back into his own lane, he cuts off the other car. The road hog seems to like making other drivers angry.

The Driver Who Is Always Right

This is the kind of driver who blames everything on someone else. Everyone makes mistakes now and then. Most people learn from their mistakes. But not this kind of driver. To hear him tell it, he *never* makes a mistake. He may get a traffic ticket for

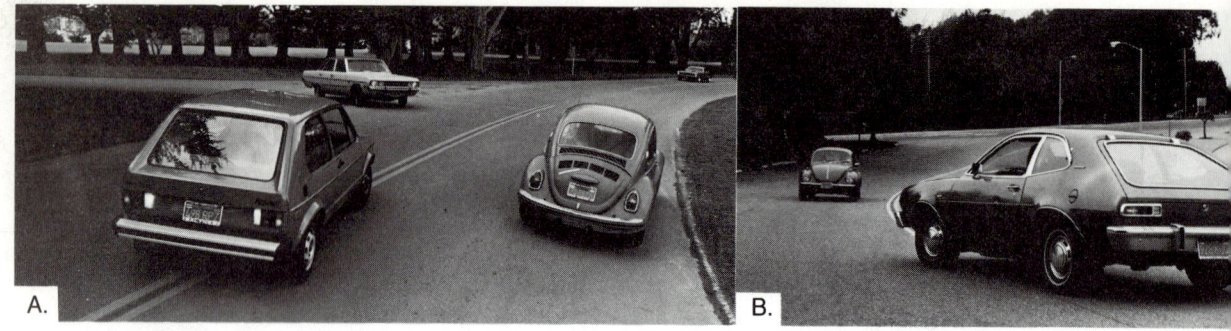

A. Passing too close to an intersection.
B. Left turn in front of oncoming car.

speeding. But he says he was not speeding. He says that the policeman was wrong. He may have an accident. But he says it was not his fault. It was the fault of the other driver. He believes it, too. No matter how foolish his driving is, he still believes he is right.

This kind of driver is dangerous because he never learns from his mistakes. He makes the same mistakes over and over again.

Spotting the Poor Driver

There are many kinds of poor driving personalities. Sometimes they are easy to spot on the road. If you can spot them, often you can stay away from them. But sometimes they are not so easy to spot. The best thing to do is to watch out for *all* other drivers. The drivers around you may be good drivers. But don't count on it. Keep ready for anything. Don't let a bad driver get you into an accident.

The Good Driving Personality

What kinds of things make for a good driving personality? First, good drivers know what they are doing. They know how to drive well. They know the traffic laws. And they know themselves.

D.

Good drivers are sure of their driving skills. But they know there is always something more about driving that they can learn. They make driving mistakes now and then. But good drivers do not blame others for their own mistakes. They try to learn from their mistakes.

Behind the wheel, good drivers keep their minds on driving. They do not turn their heads to talk to passengers in the rear seat. They do not slow down to look in store windows along the street. And, if they are driving alone, they do not get lost in their own thoughts. Good drivers keep their eye on the road at all times. And they keep their minds on their driving.

Driving is not always fun, and good drivers know it. They may get caught in heavy traffic on a hot summer day. Other drivers may be blowing their horns. But good drivers try not to become angry. They know that getting angry will not help matters.

Good drivers know that they do not own the road. They care about the rights and feelings of other drivers and pedestrians. Good drivers make sure to signal before they turn or stop. They do not push their way into traffic or cut off other drivers. If they are going slower than others, good drivers let faster cars pass. Good drivers know that when drivers help each other, traffic moves more smoothly.

C. Taking dangerous shortcut.
D. Passing too close to oncoming traffic.

Always let others know what you are going to do next. This makes driving easier and safer for everyone.

Learning To Look

A person with a good driving personality always thinks ahead. He tries to spot trouble-in-the-making while he still has time to do something about it. How good are you at thinking ahead? Can you spot trouble-in-the-making in the pictures on page 35?

Your Driving Personality

Right now, you are on your way to becoming a good driver. But you still have a long way to go. Getting your driver's license is only the first step. The more you drive, the more you will learn. The more you learn about driving, the better your driving skills will become. The more you learn about yourself, the better your driving personality will become. What kind of driving personality will you have? Only *you* can answer that.

35

Checking What You Have Read

1. What do we mean when we talk about a person's "driving personality"?
2. Being able to drive well does not mean a person has a good driving personality. Why not?
3. The show-off thinks he is a good driver. Is he? What do other people think of the way he drives?
4. Why is the hot head dangerous to himself and to other drivers?
5. How does the nervous driver cause accidents?
6. List three things the thoughtless driver might do while driving.
7. How are the driving personalities of the road hog and the thoughtless driver much the same?
8. How can a person learn from his mistakes? What happens if a person does not try to learn from his mistakes?
9. List four things that make for a good driving personality.
10. *A person with a good driving personality always thinks ahead.* What does this mean?

To Talk About

1. What kind of driving personality did Bob Lupe have? Do you think he cared more about Rita or himself? Do you think he felt sure of his driving skills?
2. A person who is sure of his driving skills feels no need to show off. Do you think a race driver needs to show off when driving on the street?
3. Some poor driving personalities are easy to spot. But others are not so easy to spot. What can you do to watch out for these kinds of drivers? What can you do when you see a poor driver ahead of you on the road?

4. Six kinds of poor driving personalities are talked about in this chapter. Can you think of any other kinds of poor driving personalities? Talk it over with others in class.

5. When other drivers help each other, traffic moves more smoothly. How can other drivers help each other? Give examples.

6. Can a person with a poor driving personality ever change? What could he do to become a better driver? What would be the *first* thing he would have to do?

Things To Do

Visit the school parking lot at the end of the school day. Watch for examples of poor driving. Write a short report about the examples you see. Are most of the drivers good drivers or bad drivers? What different kinds of driving personalities can you spot?

CHAPTER 3

Nature's Traffic Laws and Car Control

Lorrie Shafer and two of her friends were going on a picnic. It was a bright, warm Saturday morning in June. Lorrie put the picnic basket in the trunk of her car. "Do we have everything?" she asked.

"I think so," answered one of the other girls.

"Then let's go!" said Lorrie. She closed the trunk and the girls got into the car. Lorrie started the engine and they were on their way. Soon, they were out of the city on a little country road. The road was not wide, but it was paved and in good condition.

Lorrie had been driving for more than a year. She felt she was a good driver. And she was. She was sure of her driving skills. But she was still learning. She knew that there was always something more about driving to learn.

Ahead, there was a curve in the road. Lorrie slowed down before she got to the curve. The road was not banked and she knew she had to be careful. Just then,

39

a dog ran out from the side of the road. Not wanting to hit it, Lorrie put on the brakes.

But to her surprise, the car did not slow down. It went into a skid. Lorrie had learned what to do in a skid. Right away, she took her foot off the brake pedal. She turned the steering wheel in the direction the rear of the car was skidding. Before anyone had time to be afraid, Lorrie had the car back under control.

"Wow! What happened?" one of her friends asked.

"That is what I would like to know," Lorrie answered. "We skidded, but I don't know why. The road was dry. There was no water or oil on it. I was going at a safe speed. My brakes are in good condition. And my tires are almost new. But still we skidded. I want to find out why."

Lorrie pulled the car off to one side of the road. The girls got out and walked back to the curve. "Look," one of them said. "Here is why you skidded. There is sand on the road. The wind blew it here."

"Sand!" said Lorrie. "I should have seen it. But I did not. I missed one of nature's traffic signs. And because I did, I broke one of nature's traffic laws."

"Nature's traffic laws?" one of the girls asked.

"Yes," Lorrie answered. "Men make traffic laws. But so does nature."

The force of friction between your tires and the road depends on road conditions. There is much more danger of skidding in winter because of poor road conditions.

Nature's Laws

In some ways, nature's laws are like any other kind of laws. State traffic laws make driving easier and safer. They are a help to the driver. Nature's laws can also be a help to the driver. To be a good driver, you must know all the traffic laws. You must also know about nature's laws.

Friction

Nature's laws can not be changed. They are always working on you and your car. One of these laws has to do with friction. Friction is a force that tries to keep things from moving when they rub together. You can feel what friction does by rubbing your hands together. Try it. What happens? Why do your hands begin to feel warm?

Under some conditions there is a lot of friction. Under other conditions, there is not as much friction. If you have ever used a sled in winter, you know this. A sled slides easily over snow-covered ground. There is not much friction between the sled and the snow. If there is no snow, the sled will not slide easily. There is much more friction between the sled and the ground.

When you drive, friction can help you. There is friction between your tires and the road. Without it, you would not be able to get moving. Your rear wheels would just spin around and around. Sometimes this happens. A car may get stuck in mud, snow, or ice. There is not enough friction for the car to get started.

Without friction, you would not be able to keep your car under control. Friction is needed to start, keep moving, turn, and stop your car. When you

There must be friction between the tires and the road for a car to start moving.

The points of friction between the tires and road are small. This is why a car with worn tires skids so easily.

Friction is needed for stopping a car.

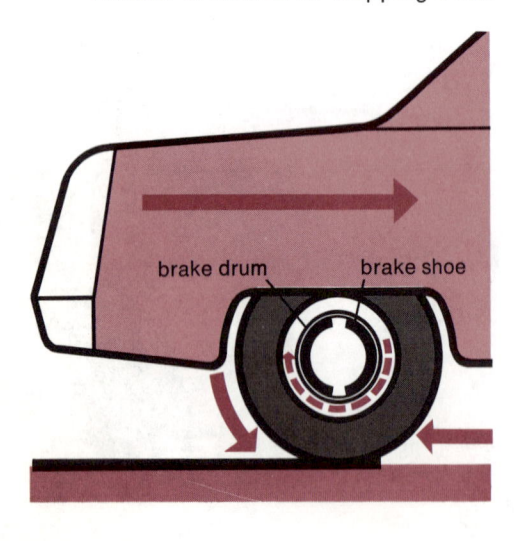

brake drum   brake shoe

push on the brake pedal, the brake shoe rubs against the brake drum. Friction between the brake shoe and the brake drum slows the wheel. Friction between the tire and the road then slows the car down. At last, because of this friction, the car stops.

Always make sure your brakes and tires are in good condition. If your brakes are worn, you do not have as much friction. You can not stop as fast. The condition of your tires is just as important. There should be plenty of tread on them. If the tread is worn, there is not as much friction. A car with worn tires takes much more time to stop. And a car with worn tires can easily skid.

The friction that keeps your car in the right place on the road is not always the same. Water, snow, ice, oil, or wet leaves all cut down on friction. If you try to speed up, the tires may spin. If you turn too fast, the car may slide off the road. You have to use the brakes gently, and allow more room to stop. If you slam the brakes on, the car may slide out of control. On slippery roads, the careful, slow driver does okay. The fast driver may have an accident. In snow country, you may have to put chains on.

Centrifugal Force

Another of nature's laws has to do with centrifugal force. This force acts on all moving things. Centrifugal force tries to keep things moving in a straight line.

You can see how centrifugal force works. Roll a piece of paper into a ball. Then tie a string to it. Now swing the paper around and around. What happens? How does the paper move? Let go of the string. What happens to the paper? Does it keep moving around? Or does it go off in a straight line?

Centrifugal force is at work when you are turning or rounding a curve. This force tries to keep your car going straight. It tries to push your car off the road. You are able to turn because of the force of friction. Friction between your tires and the road makes the car turn.

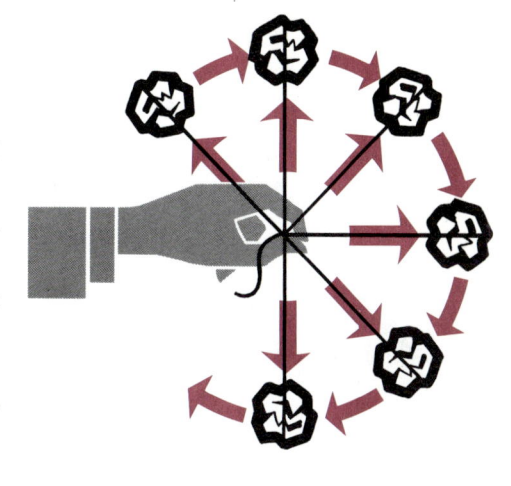

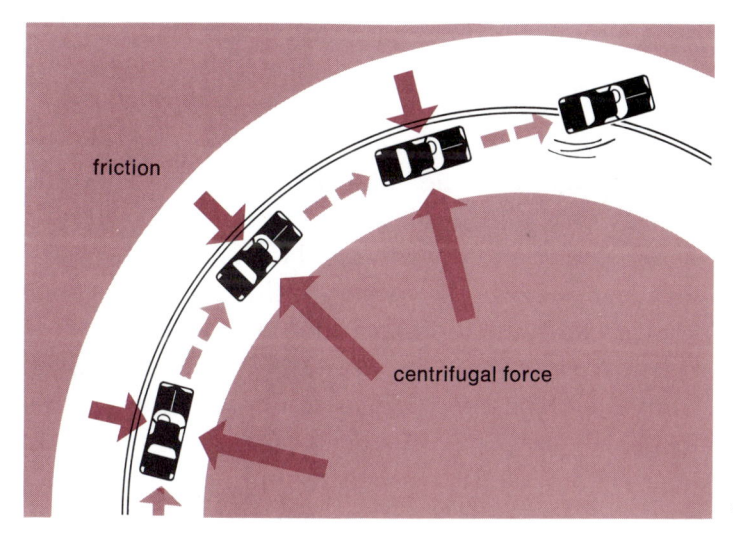

If there is more centrifugal force than friction, a car will begin to skid.

Friction acts against centrifugal force. As long as there is more friction than centrifugal force, you can turn. But if there is more centrifugal force than friction, your car slides off the road.

The control a driver has when rounding a curve depends on these things:

- speed of the car
- sharpness of the curve
- tire and road condition
- how the road is made

Speed

The faster a car rounds a curve, the more centrifugal force pushes against it. If you try to round a curve going too fast, you can skid. The car may slide off the road and even turn over.

When nearing a curve, watch for road signs. Often there will be a sign telling the safe speed for the curve ahead. Do not try to round the curve any faster than the speed on the sign. Even if there is no sign, you may still want to slow down. Do not drive any faster than you think is safe.

Tire and Road Condition

Only a small part of each tire presses against the road at any one time. The part that presses on the road is only a little bigger than your hand. Here is where the friction is you need to control your car—four small spots. The friction of the tires acts against centrifugal force to keep you on the road.

But if your tires are worn, there is not as much friction. It does not take as much centrifugal force to push your car off the road. The same thing can happen if the road is wet. Rounding a curve on a wet day can be dangerous even with new tires.

Sharpness of the Curve

How much centrifugal force there is also depends on the sharpness of the curve. The sharper the curve, the more centrifugal force there can be. You can cut down on the centrifugal force by slowing your car. On a sharp curve, you may have to go very slow.

How the Road Is Made

The way the road is made is also important. There are three kinds of road curves.

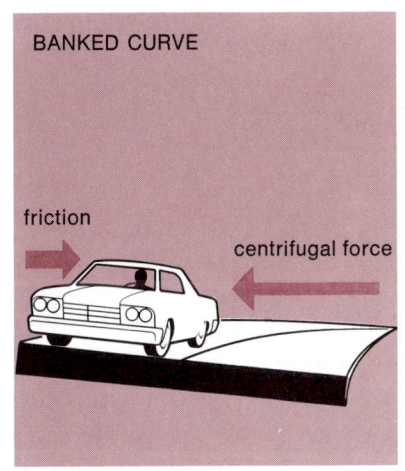

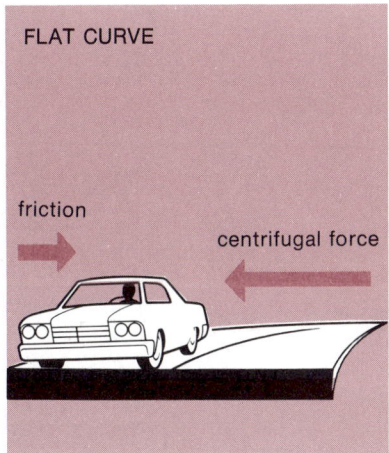

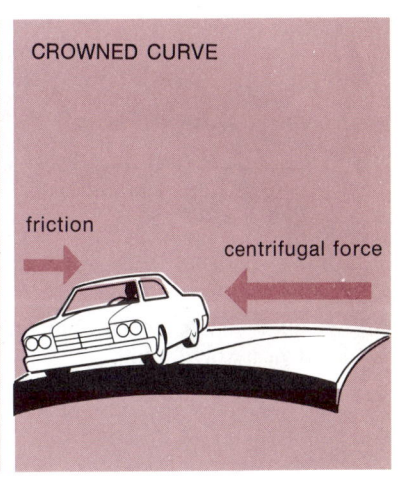

The banked curve is the best. The way the road is made helps keep cars on the road. Centrifugal force can not push a car off so easily.

The flat curve is not as safe. Rounding a flat curve at high speed is dangerous. A driver must slow down before rounding this kind of curve.

The crowned curve is the most dangerous. A driver on the outside of a crowned curve must go slow. If he does not, centrifugal force will push him off the road.

Gravity

Gravity is a force that pulls things to the ground. Throw a ball into the air. It goes up. But then it comes back down. Gravity brings it down. Jump off

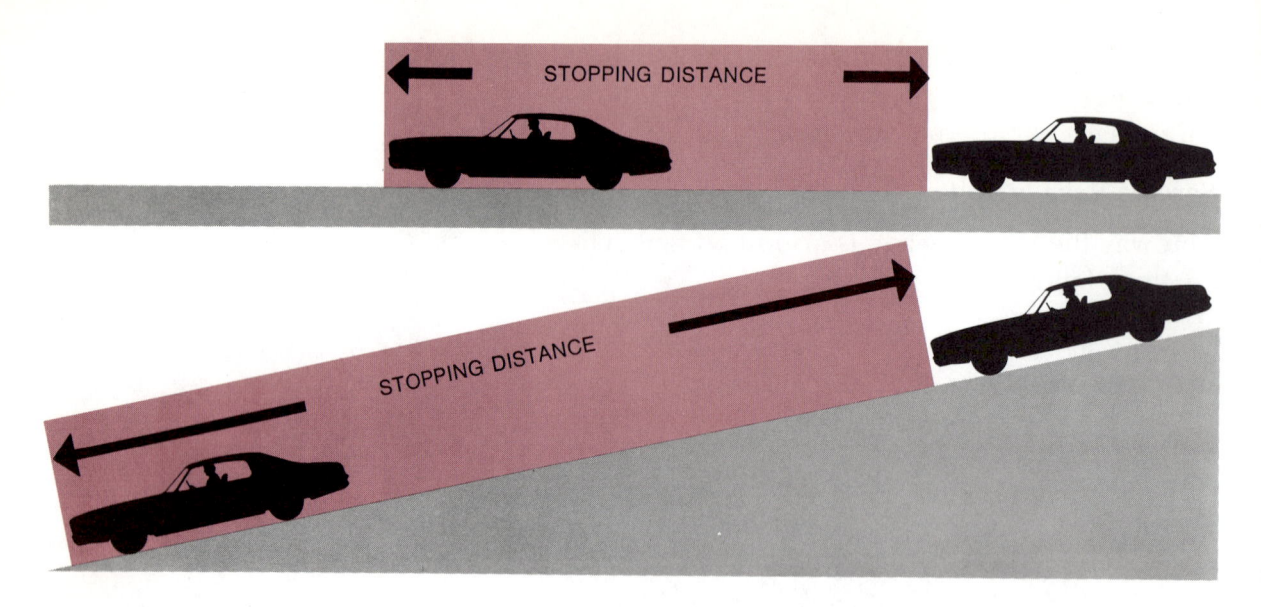

You need much more stopping distance when driving down a hill.

the ground. Gravity brings you right back. Gravity pulls more on heavy things than on light things. The pull of gravity on a car—a very heavy thing—can be quite strong. You must keep this in mind when you drive.

When you drive up a hill, the pull of gravity slows your car. To keep going at the same speed, you must give the engine more gas. When you are going down a hill, gravity also pulls on your car. The pull of gravity makes the car go faster.

Going down a hill, you need more room to stop. At 40 mph on a flat road, you can stop your car in 145 feet. Going down a hill at the same speed, you might need 245 feet to stop.

As you start going down a hill, take your foot off the accelerator. By doing this, your engine will act as a brake. Watch your speed. Use your brakes from time to time to keep the car at a safe speed. But do not keep your foot on the brakes all the time. Let your engine help slow the car. On some hills, you may have to change to a lower gear.

Force of Impact

No one wants to have an accident. No one wants to run into something with his car. But accidents do happen. And the good driver knows what happens in an accident. He knows about another of nature's laws—the force of impact. Impact means how hard one thing hits another. The more impact there is, the more damage is done. The force of impact depends on four things:

- the speed of the moving car
- the "give" of the thing that is hit
- the weight of the moving car
- the weight of the thing that is hit

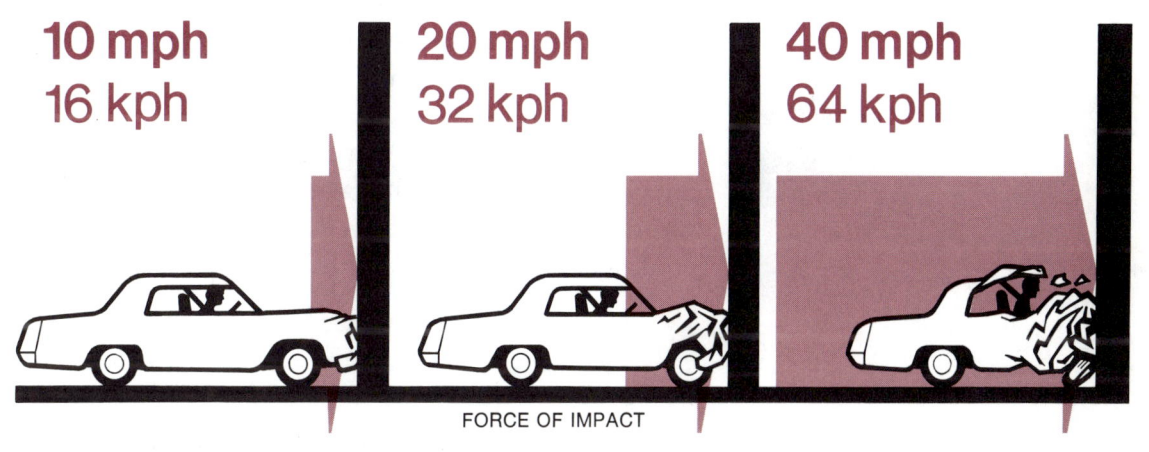

10 mph
16 kph

20 mph
32 kph

40 mph
64 kph

FORCE OF IMPACT

Impact and Speed

The faster a car is moving when it hits something, the more impact there is. Suppose a car going 10 mph hits a tree. Now suppose another car going 20 mph hits a tree. This car was going twice as fast. But the force of impact is not twice as much. It is four times as much. At 40 mph, the force of impact would be 16 times as much.

Impact and "Give"

If a car hits a large tree, the car stops all at once. There is little or no "give." Because of this, the impact is great. There is much damage to the car. Suppose another car, going at the same speed, runs into some bushes. The bushes have much more "give." The car knocks down one bush after another. As it hits each bush, it slows a little. At last, it stops. The car is not damaged much because of the "give" of the bushes.

Impact and Weight

The more a thing weighs, the more impact it has if it hits something. Suppose a pedestrian is hit by a bicycle going 10 mph. The pedestrian might not be hurt. But suppose he is hit by a car going at the same speed. Because of the car's weight, the force of impact would be much more. The pedestrian might even be killed.

People inside a car can also be hurt because of impact. A person might be thrown into the windshield. To keep this from happening, always use your seat belt when driving. Ask your passengers to do the same.

Stopping Distance

When driving, you must be ready to stop at any time. Suppose a child runs out into the street in front of your car. You see the danger and decide to stop. You hit the brakes as hard as you can. The car slows. But it does not stop all at once. How much stopping distance will you need?

Stopping distance depends on three things:

1. The time it takes you to see the danger and decide to stop.

2. The time it takes you to get your foot to the brake pedal. This is called the *reaction time*. The distance your car covers in this time is called the *reaction distance*.

3. The time it takes for the brakes to stop the car. This is called the *braking time*. The distance your car covers in this time is called the *braking distance*.

A good driver is quick to spot danger ahead. He keeps his mind on his driving and his eyes on the road. The good driver thinks ahead. He tries to spot trouble-in-the-making. But even the best driver can not keep a child from running into the street. His stopping distance then depends on his reaction distance and his braking distance.

**Reaction Distance + Braking Distance
= Stopping Distance**

Reaction Time and Distance

You spot danger and decide to stop. How long does it take before you react? How long does it take to get your foot on the brake pedal? The reaction time of most drivers is about ¾ of a second. This is not very long. But in this short time, the car keeps going. The distance it covers depends on the speed of the car. The faster the car is going, the more distance it covers. At 20 mph, the reaction distance is about 22 feet. At 60 mph, the reaction distance is three times as much. Your car moves 66 feet—and you still have not slowed one bit.

Braking Time and Distance

Once you push the brake pedal, the car begins to slow. How many more feet will you go before the car stops? The braking distance depends on how fast you are going. At 20 mph, the braking distance is 22 feet. The braking distance at 60 mph is more than nine times as much. Your car moves almost 200 feet before it stops.

The table shows stopping distance under the best conditions. Under conditions that are not as good you need more room to stop. You need more room if:

- the road is wet or slippery
- your tires or brakes are worn
- your reaction time is slow

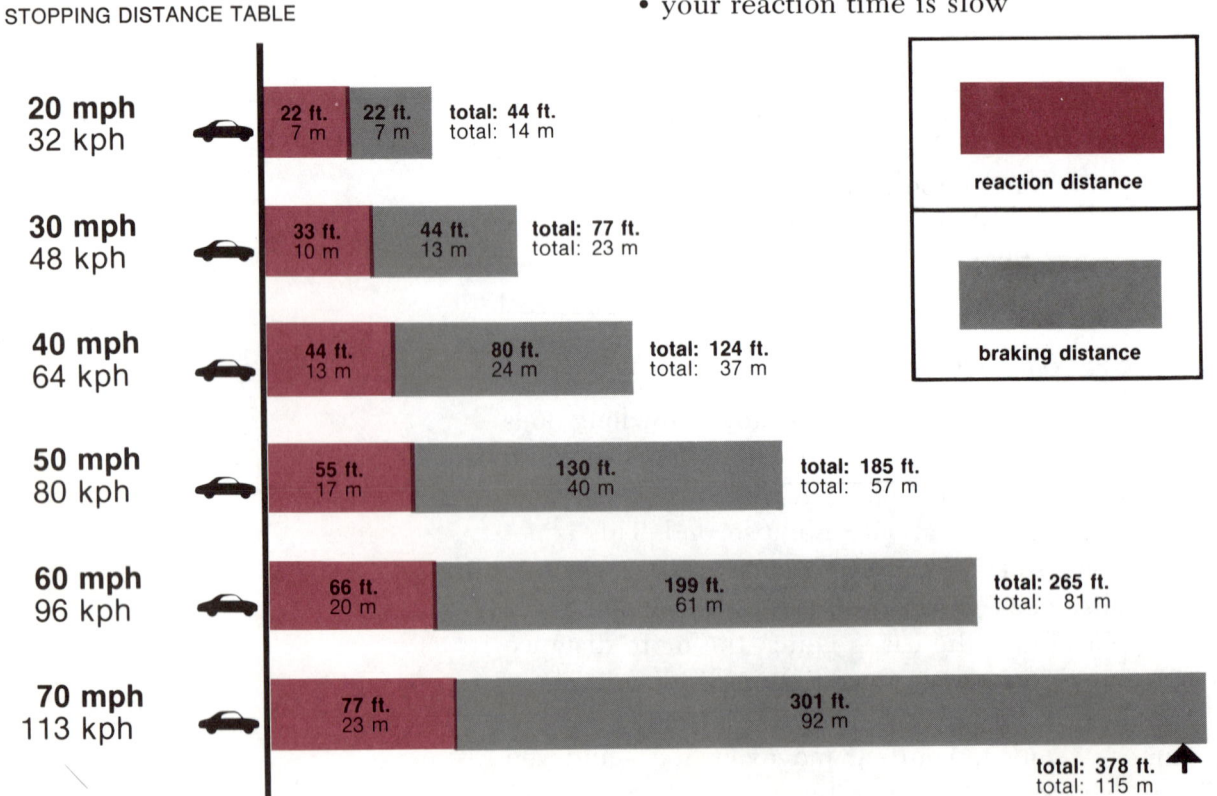

STOPPING DISTANCE TABLE

Speed	Reaction Distance	Braking Distance	Total
20 mph / 32 kph	22 ft. / 7 m	22 ft. / 7 m	44 ft. / 14 m
30 mph / 48 kph	33 ft. / 10 m	44 ft. / 13 m	77 ft. / 23 m
40 mph / 64 kph	44 ft. / 13 m	80 ft. / 24 m	124 ft. / 37 m
50 mph / 80 kph	55 ft. / 17 m	130 ft. / 40 m	185 ft. / 57 m
60 mph / 96 kph	66 ft. / 20 m	199 ft. / 61 m	265 ft. / 81 m
70 mph / 113 kph	77 ft. / 23 m	301 ft. / 92 m	378 ft. / 115 m

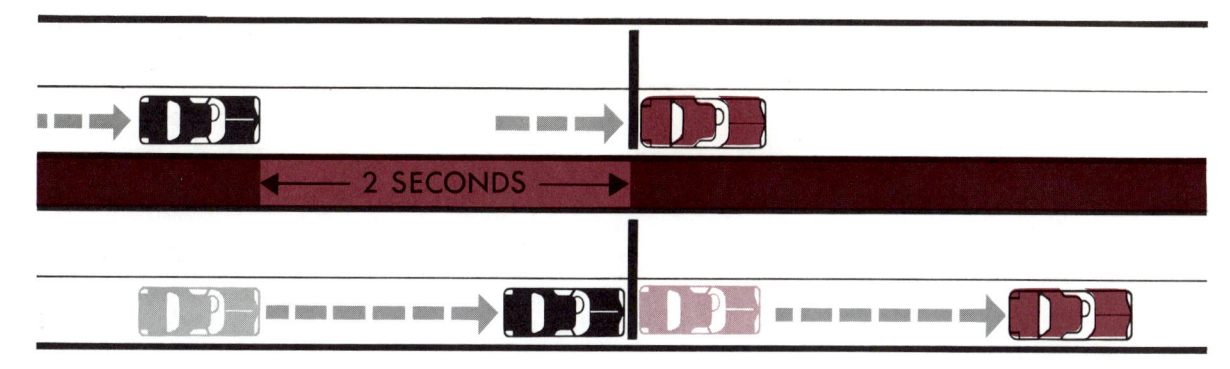

Safe Following Distances

In traffic, always leave enough room between your car and the car ahead. Following another car too closely can be dangerous. Suppose the first car begins to stop. You see his brake lights go on. You react. But ¾ of a second goes by before your foot gets to the brake pedal. The other car is already slowing down. If you are following too closely, you may not be able to stop in time. Your stopping distance may be too great.

What is a safe following distance? That depends on how fast you are going. The faster you are going, the more your following distance should be. For every 10 mph, leave one car length between your car and the car ahead. For example, at 20 mph leave two car lengths. At 50 mph, leave five car lengths. Under poor road conditions, you may need to leave even more room than this.

Judging a safe following distance is not always easy. The best way to do it is to use the Two-Second Rule. Watch the car ahead of you. Note when the rear of that car passes over a certain point on the road. (The point might be a shadow, a painted road marking, or the like.) As the car ahead passes this point, begin counting: "One-thousand-and-one, one-thousand-and-two." It should take you about

The driver of the black car keeps a safe following distance by using the Two-Second Rule. He stays two seconds behind the car ahead of him.

two seconds to finish counting. If the front of your car gets to the point before you finish, you are too close.

Nature's Traffic Laws

Many drivers do not know much about nature's laws. Some drivers even think they can get away with breaking nature's laws. But the good driver knows that this can not be done. Nature's laws are always at work. The good driver keeps this in mind when he drives. He follows the traffic laws made by man. He also follows nature's traffic laws.

Checking What You Have Read

1. What do we mean when we say that nature's laws can not be changed?
2. Why must there always be some friction between a car's tires and the road? What happens when there is not enough friction?
3. Why is it dangerous to drive a car that has worn tires?
4. When there is water on the road, there is danger of skidding. List four more road conditions where there is danger of skidding.
5. How does centrifugal force act on a car going round a curve?
6. What force acts *against* centrifugal force?
7. The control a driver has when rounding a curve depends on four things. What are these four things?
8. Why is a banked curve the safest kind of curve?
9. How does the force of gravity act on a car going down a hill?
10. What can a driver do to keep from going down a hill too fast? List three things he can do.

11. The force of impact depends on four things. What are these four things?
12. Which has more "give," a large tree or a row of bushes?
13. Suppose a driver is not wearing his seat belt. And suppose his car runs into a tree. What could happen?
14. What is reaction time? What is reaction distance?
15. What do road conditions have to do with stopping distance? What does rain, for example, have to do with how long it takes to stop a car?
16. What is the Two-Second Rule? How do you use it?

To Talk About

1. Rows of bushes are often planted along the sides of freeways and other roads. Why do you suppose these bushes have been planted? Would it be better to plant trees along the roads?
2. *Brakes don't stop a car. Brakes stop the wheels of a car.* Why is it important to keep this in mind when driving on wet or slippery roads?

Things To Do

Ride in a car with a licensed driver. Test the Two-Second Rule at 35 mph. Then test it at 45 mph and 55 mph. Does the rule work the same at different speeds? Write a short report on what you find out.

Test the reaction time of students in your class. Ask your teacher to help with the testing. Is everyone's reaction time the same? Or do some students have faster reaction times? (Reaction times in class will be faster than reaction times when driving. Why is this so?) Write a report on reaction times. What does physical condition have to do with reaction time? Does alcohol change a person's reaction time? Do drugs slow a person's reaction time?

CHAPTER **4**

Traffic Laws and You

It was late at night. There were only a few lights on in the houses along the street. Most people were sleeping. But not Larry Gold. He worked nights. And now, his night's work over, he was driving home. There was a stop sign at the intersection ahead. Larry slowed down but did not stop. After all, there were not many people driving at this time of night.

He had not gone far when he saw a flashing red light behind him. "The police," he said to himself. Larry pulled the car over and stopped. The police car stopped in front of him and a policeman got out.

"May I see your license, please?" the policeman said.

Larry handed his driver's license to the policeman. "Is there something wrong?" he asked.

"Did you see that stop sign at the intersection?" the policeman asked

"Sure I did," said Larry. "I drive this way every night coming home from work. I live just down the street."

"Then you know you are supposed to stop at that intersection," said the policeman.

"On my way to work, I always *do* stop," Larry answered. "There is a lot of traffic then. But I don't see much point in stopping at this time of night. You are not going to give me a ticket for this, are you?"

"Yes, I am," said the policeman. "But before I do, let me tell you why. You said you don't see much point in stopping at that intersection. But there are some good reasons for doing so. First of all, if you *had* stopped, you would not be getting this ticket. But there are much better reasons than that.

"Take another look at the intersection tomorrow. It is a four-way stop. You did not stop because you were sure no other cars were coming. But what if another car *was* coming? And what if that driver, like you, also did not see any point in stopping? Both of you might have been killed. And for what? How much time did you save by not stopping? Not even a minute."

"I had not thought about it like that before," said Larry.

The policeman began writing the traffic ticket. "Traffic laws make driving safer and easier for all of us," he said. "But laws are not much good if they are not followed. They have to be followed day *and* night. Suppose all drivers followed the laws only when they felt like it? Now do you begin to get the point?"

Larry smiled. "Yes. I get the point. But I wish I was not getting the ticket."

"I know," said the policeman. "Getting a ticket is a hard way to have to learn something. But look at it this way. Do you think having an accident would be a better way?"

Knowing the Law

The laws of nature are always at work. These laws do not need the police to see that they are followed. Good drivers know that they cannot get away with breaking nature's laws. They know they must follow these laws for their own safety. Good drivers feel the same way about their state's traffic laws. They know that traffic laws make driving safer for everyone. Traffic laws make driving easier, too. They help traffic move better.

Before you apply for your driver's license, you must know your state's traffic laws. To learn about the laws in your state, you will need a vehicle code book. You can get this book from your state's Department of Motor Vehicles.

Traffic laws are not the same in every state. But all states have some laws that are the same. These laws are the "rules of the road" all across our land. Here are some of the most important of these rules.

Right-of-Way

Suppose two cars are coming to an intersection from different directions. Right-of-way laws tell us which car can go ahead and which car must yield.

1. A car on a through street has the right-of-way. A car coming from a side street must yield.//
2. A car already in an intersection has the right-of-way. The other car must yield.
3. Two cars may get to an intersection at the same time. When this happens, the car on the right has the right-of-way.
4. A car going straight ahead has the right-of-way over a car turning left.
5. A pedestrian in a crosswalk has the right-of-way over all cars. Drivers must yield to pedestrians in crosswalks.
6. Emergency vehicles such as fire engines, ambulances, and police cars always have the right-of-way. You can tell when an emergency vehicle is coming. Sometimes you will see a flashing red light. Or you may hear a siren. When you see an emergency vehicle coming, pull over to the right and stop.

Driver Signals

Other drivers and pedestrians must know what you are going to do. Before you stop or make a turn, you must signal. For turns, you can use the turn signals in your car. You can also signal with your left arm. Today's cars all have turn signals. But you must still know how to signal with your arm. If your turn signals break, you may have to give arm signals.

RIGHT TURN

LEFT TURN

SLOW OR STOP

59

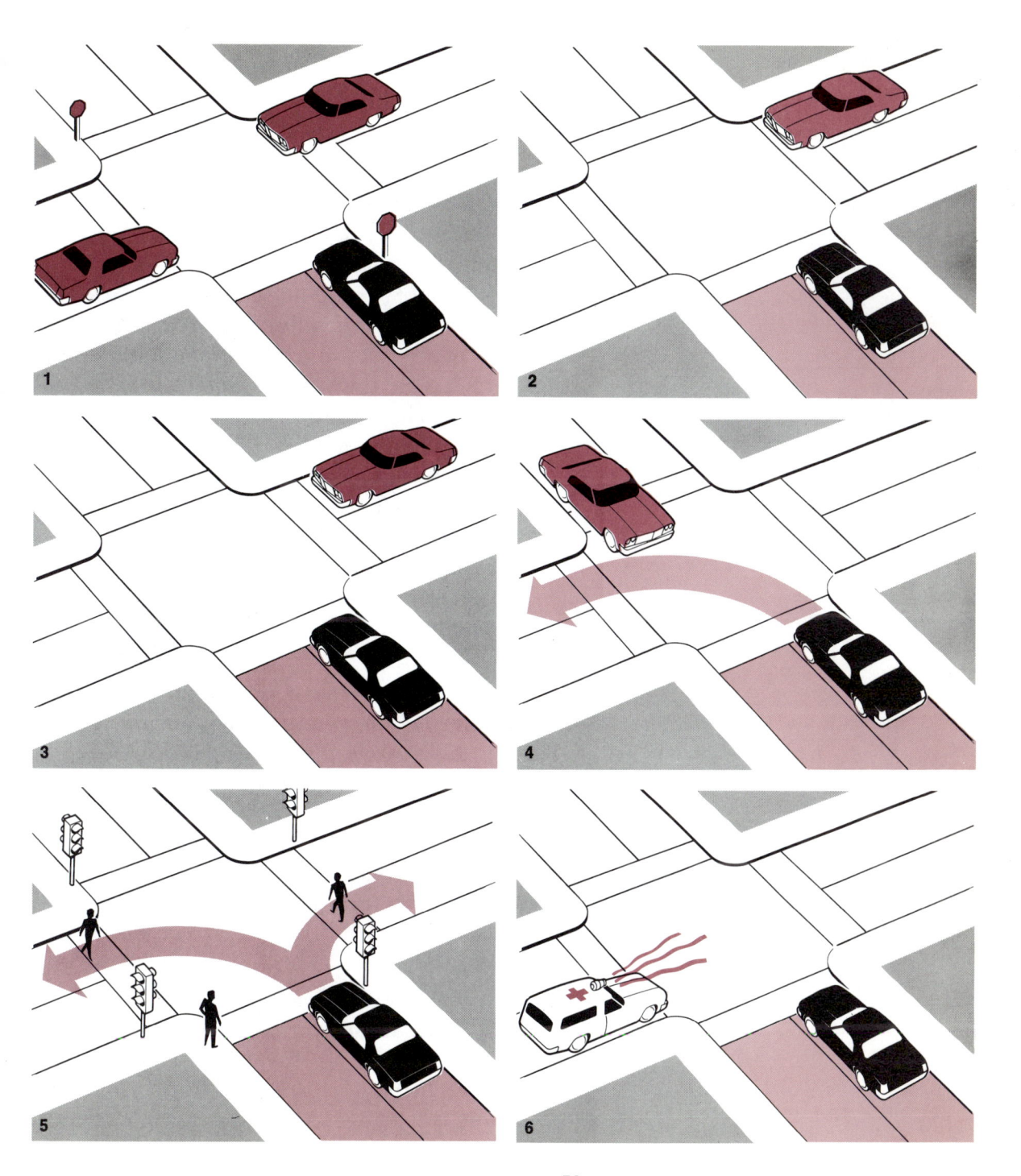

Traffic Signals

At busy intersections traffic signals are used. Most drivers call traffic signals "stop lights." Traffic signals keep traffic moving by controlling the right-of-way. Traffic signals tell drivers when to go and when to wait.

The red light is always on the top.* It means stop. The yellow light, in the middle, means the signal is changing. When the yellow light comes on, drivers must get ready to stop. The green light, on the bottom, means go. It gives you the right-of-way. But even when you have the green light, always be careful. Now and then, a car may "run the red light." He should stop. But he does not. Look to your left and right before crossing an intersection. Also watch out for pedestrians.

Sometimes there is another light on the traffic signal. It is an arrow pointing left or right. When this light comes on, you may turn in the direction the arrow is pointing.

Not all traffic signals have a red, yellow, and green light. At intersections where there is not much traffic a flashing light is often used. A flashing red light means stop. If no cars are coming from the left or right, you may then go.

If the signal is a flashing yellow light, you do not have to stop. But you must slow down. Look both ways before going through the intersection. Be sure the way is clear.

Most traffic signals have the lights from top to bottom, as in the picture on this page. In some traffic signals, however, the lights may be from left to right. In these signals, red is always on the left. Yellow is in the middle. Green is on the right.

Road Signs

Road signs are a big help to drivers. Road signs tell drivers what to do and what to look for. Without signs, drivers would have a hard time knowing what was ahead. Drivers would not always know what the safe speed limit was.

Each kind of sign has a different shape. Before you can get a driver's license, you must know what each shape means. You must be able to tell what a sign means by its shape alone. Look at the five shapes here. How many shapes do you know the meaning of?

Shapes and Meaning

The five most important kinds of signs are: stop sign, warning sign, railroad crossing sign, yield sign, and regulatory sign. Each of these signs has its own shape.

Stop Sign

The stop sign has 8 sides. It is the only sign with this shape. It is always red with white letters. When coming to a stop sign, be sure to make a full stop. Do not start up again until you are sure the way is clear.

Warning Signs

Most warning signs are diamond-shaped. They are yellow and black. Warning signs tell the driver there may be danger ahead. Some warning signs tell what the danger may be with words. On other warning signs, there are no words. The sign *shows* what the danger may be. The sign is a kind of picture. To drive safely, you must learn what each of these warning signs means.

61

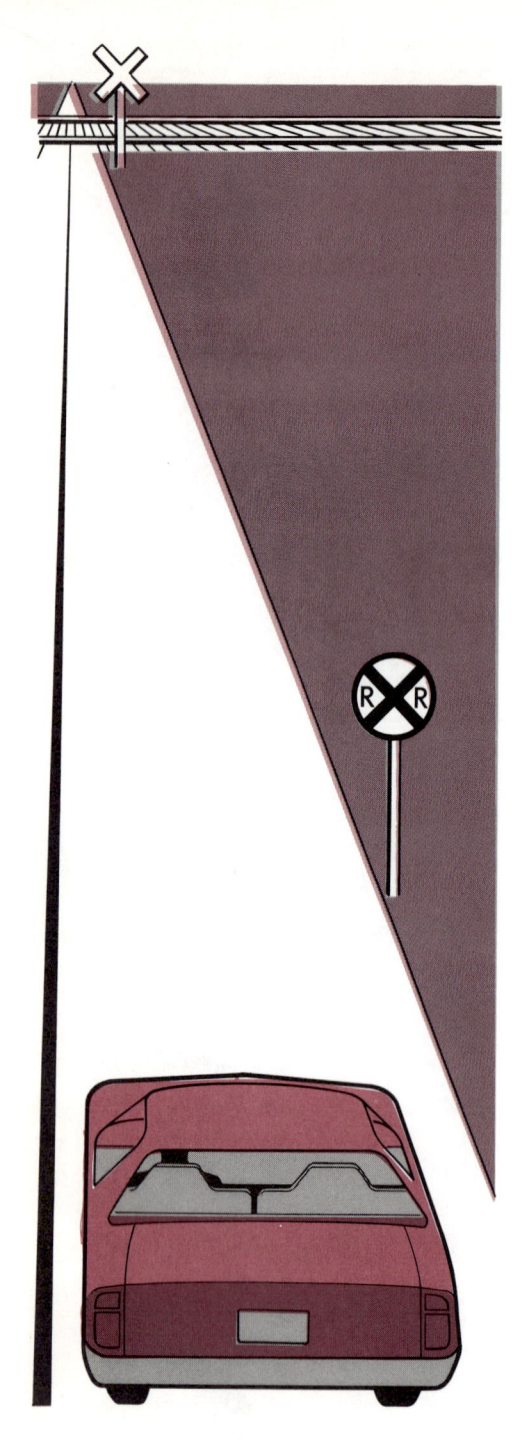

Railroad Crossing Signs

A round sign means there is a railroad crossing ahead. The two *R*s stand for "railroad." When you get near the tracks, there may be other warnings, too. At some railroad crossings, a gate comes down to stop traffic when a train is coming. At other crossings, a ringing bell and flashing light may warn of a coming train.

Sometimes, there is only an X-shaped sign. This sign is always close to the tracks. It tells how many tracks there are. Always slow down before crossing railroad tracks. Make sure no train is coming on *any* of the tracks.

Yield Sign

At some intersections there is a triangle-shaped sign. This triangle shape is used for only one kind of sign—the yield sign. A yield sign means that you do not have the right-of-way. You must give way to the cars that have the right-of-way. You may have to slow down or even stop. When the way is clear, you may go on.

Regulatory and Information Signs

Regulatory signs always have four sides. Regulatory signs tell about traffic laws. Speed limit signs are regulatory signs, for example. Information signs tell about places and conditions ahead. They may tell how far it is to the next town, for example.

Road Markings

Road markings are another help to the driver. Broken white lines show where the lanes are. These lines help drivers stay in their own lane. The center line on two-lane roads is also a broken white line. You can cross this kind of line to pass or turn. But be sure it is safe before you do so.

On city streets, the center line may be a solid line. It may be white or yellow. Try to keep from crossing this line. Cross it only if you must.

On highways, sometimes there is a double center line. Both lines are white or yellow. The lines may both be solid. Or one may be a broken line. If the broken line is in your lane, you can cross the line to pass. But if the solid line is in your lane, you must not cross it. If both lines in a double center line are solid, no one can pass. You may cross a double yellow line only to make a left turn. But you must wait until it is safe to do so. You do not have the right-of-way.

Other Painted Markings

There are many other kinds of road markings. Crosswalk lines show where pedestrians may cross. Crosswalk lines are painted on the street only at busy intersections. At intersections where they are not painted, the crosswalk is still there.

Stop lines show where you should stop your car at traffic signals. They are white or yellow lines that come out from the curb. Painted arrows show which lanes you can turn from. These are often used at busy intersections.

The Laws in Your State

The "rules of the road" we have looked at are the same in all states. But there are many other traffic laws that you must know about. Each state has its own set of laws. You can learn about the laws in your state by reading your vehicle code book. Your state may have some laws that are different from the laws in other states. In some states, for example, you may turn right at a red light after stopping. You do not have to wait for the light to turn green. In other states, this is against the law. You must know all the traffic laws in your own state. If you drive into other states, you must know the laws there, too.

Stop signs are not always easy to spot. Parked cars can hide them from view. For added safety, at many intersections the word STOP is also painted on the street.

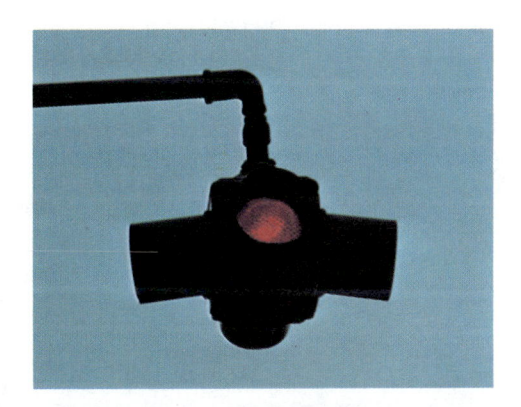

A flashing red light means the same as a stop sign. Drivers must come to a full stop. Most busy intersections are controlled with traffic signals, *right.* The red light, which means stop, is always at the top. The yellow light, in the middle, means get ready to stop. The green light, at the bottom, means go if the way is clear.

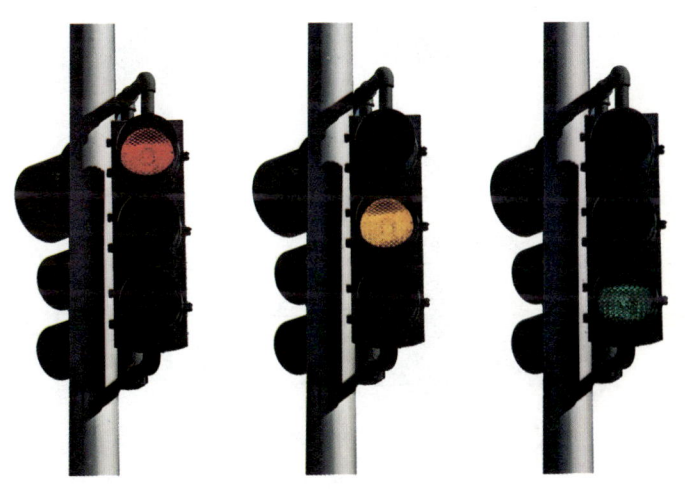

Warning signs tell drivers what the road is like ahead. Most warning signs are black and yellow. The yield sign is red and white. It is shaped like a triangle. The yield sign is the only sign that has this shape.

SLOW

Most railroad crossings are well marked. But no matter how well marked a crossing is, drivers should still be careful. Always look both ways before crossing.

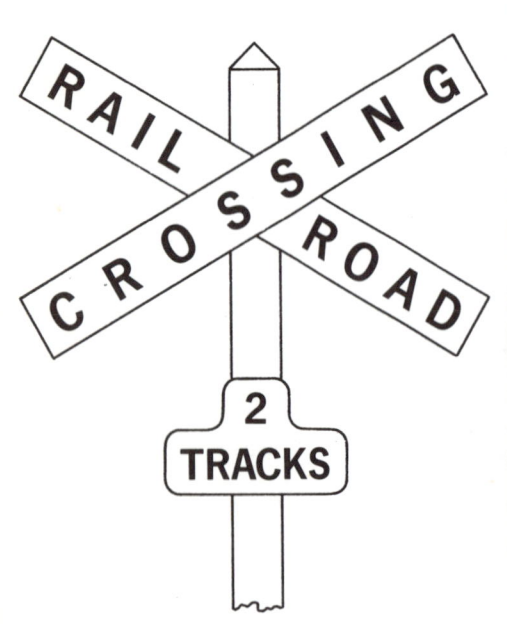

68

A driver who mistakes a freeway exit road for an entrance road is in great danger. To keep this from happening, large signs warn drivers not to enter.

Regulatory signs tell about traffic laws. These signs help keep traffic moving safely and smoothly. Information signs tell about places and conditions. They help drivers to plan ahead.

Painted road markings show drivers where the lanes are. They also warn drivers when it is not safe to pass. A solid double line always means no passing.

71

Newer road signs use symbols or pictures to show what they mean. These signs also tell what they mean in words. But, in a few years, when everyone understands the new signs, the words will be taken off. Just the symbols will be used.

Road signs give drivers important information about places and conditions ahead. They help make driving easier and safer.

Checking What You Have Read _____

1. Why do we need traffic laws? Give two reasons.
2. Suppose two cars get to an intersection at the same time. Which car has the right-of-way?
3. Suppose you are about to turn left at an intersection. Another car is coming toward you from the other direction. Who has the right-of-way?
4. Suppose you are coming to an intersection. You have the green light. Then you hear a siren. What should you do?
5. Today's cars all have turn signals. But the law says that drivers must still know how to make hand signals. Why?
6. What does the yellow light in a traffic signal mean?
7. What does a flashing red light signal mean?
8. What does an 8-sided road sign always mean? What color is this sign?
9. What does a round sign always mean? What color is this sign?
10. What do diamond-shaped signs mean? What color are these signs?
11. What does a triangle-shaped sign mean? What color is this sign?
12. What does an X-shaped sign always mean? What color is this sign?
13. What are regulatory signs? What kinds of things do they tell drivers?
14. What does a solid double-yellow center line painted on the road mean?
15. Suppose there are no crosswalk lines painted at an intersection. Does this mean there is no crosswalk at the intersection?

To Talk About

1. Some drivers do not stop for traffic signals when there is no one around. What is wrong with doing this kind of thing? What could happen?
2. Most states have what is called a "basic speed law." It says that drivers should drive at a speed safe for conditions. Suppose you are driving on a road with a posted speed limit of 45 mph. Under what conditions would 45 mph be too fast?
3. What is the reason for having yield signs? Why not just use stop signs?
4. Most international road signs do not have any writing on them. These signs use pictures to show conditions. Do you think international road signs are better than the ones we are now using? Why or why not? What kind of signs do you think are best?

Things To Do

Find out about the vehicle code in your state. What are the penalties for breaking different traffic laws? For what reasons will the state take away a person's driver's license? Visit the traffic court in your town. How many drivers are in court for speeding? How many are there for other reasons? Write a short report on what you find out.

CHAPTER 5

What Are Your Driver Responsibilities?

It was over almost before Art Mendez knew what was happening. The intersection looked clear. He did not see the other car until it was too late. Art hit his brakes as hard as he could. But there was not enough time to stop. His car skidded into the side of the other car. There was a loud bang and both cars came to a stop. Art took off his seat belt and got out of his car. The other driver also got out of his car.

"Are you hurt?" Art asked.

"No. I am all right," the man answered. "How about you?"

"I think I am all right, too," Art said.

The two men looked at the damage. The front of Art's car was pushed in. The side of the other car was also pushed in. A woman who had seen the accident walked over to the men. "I live just up the street," she said. "Is there anything I can do?"

"Yes," said Art. "Would you please call the police? You can tell them that no one has been hurt."

Art got some paper from his car. First, he put down the license plate number of the other car. Then he took his driver's license from his pocket. "May I see your driver's license, please?" he asked. "Here is mine."

Art began writing down the name and address of the other driver. The other man also got some paper and began writing. "Do you have insurance?" the man asked.

"Yes," Art answered. "Do you?"

"Yes, I have insurance, too," the man told Art. "Funny. I never thought I would need it. I always though accidents only happened to *other* people."

"Me too," said Art. "But now *we* are the other people."

Accidents and the Law

No one wants to have an accident. But accidents *do* happen. Even the best driver can not say he will never have an accident. If he does have an accident, he knows what to do. Here are six things the law says you *must* do:

1. Stop your car at once.
2. Help anyone who may have been hurt in the accident.
3. Send for an ambulance, if one is needed.
4. Give your name, address, and license plate number to the other driver. Show him your driver's license. Ask the other driver for the same information.
5. Report the accident to the police.
6. Send a written report of the accident to the state Motor Vehicle Department. (You will also want to send a written report of the accident to your insurance company.)

Laws about accidents are not the same in every state. In some states, you must pull your car off the road if you can. In other states, you must not move your car until after the police have come. Make sure you know the laws in your state.

If your car can not be moved, warn other drivers there has been an accident. Often one accident causes another accident. Other drivers may not be able to see that the road is blocked. Let them know there is danger ahead so no one will run into your car. At night, use flares. You should always carry flares in your car.

If someone has been hurt, give what help you can. Stop bleeding by pressing on the cut. Keep the person warm. But do not try to move the person. You could hurt him even more by trying to move him. Call a doctor and the police as soon as you can.

Many drivers carry accident report forms with them in their cars. If a driver is in an accident, he will know which questions to ask. He can get all the information he needs while things are still fresh in his mind.

Write down as much information about the accident as you can. Get the name, address, and license plate number of the other driver. Also write down the make and year of his car. Make a note of how much damage was done to each car.

Get the names and addresses of any people who saw the accident. Write down the time of day the accident happened. Tell about road conditions. Make a drawing showing how the accident happened. Your insurance company will need this information. Keep an accident report with you in your car. If you have an accident, the accident report will help you know what questions to ask.

Insurance

The law says that a driver is responsible for his or her driving. If a person causes an accident, the person must be ready to answer for it. If a driver damages another car, the law says the driver must pay for the damage. If a driver hurts or kills someone, the driver must be ready to answer for that, too.

Because a driver is responsible for his or her driving, he or she should have automobile insurance. All drivers should have automobile insurance. You should have insurance if you own a car. You should have insurance if you drive the family car. Any car you drive should be covered by insurance.

Insurance is a way of paying for the cost of accidents. Suppose a person has an accident that causes $5,000 damage. Most people do not have $5,000 to pay for an accident. But if the person has insurance, his insurance company will pay. Here is how it works.

Let's say 100 drivers want automobile insurance. Each driver pays the insurance company $200. All together, the insurance company gets $20,000. Now suppose one of the drivers has an accident. The insurance company uses part of the $20,000 to pay for the accident. It still has money left to pay for other accidents.

There are many insurance companies. Each company sells insurance to thousands of drivers. Because of this, the companies have enough money to pay for the accidents that happen.

There are many kinds of insurance. You should know about each kind. Then, when you go to buy insurance, you will know what kind you need. Here are some of the most important kinds of automobile insurance:

1. **Bodily Injury Liability Insurance** There are two kinds of liability insurance. The first kind is called *bodily injury* liability insurance. If you hurt or kill someone with your car, you can be

comprehensive

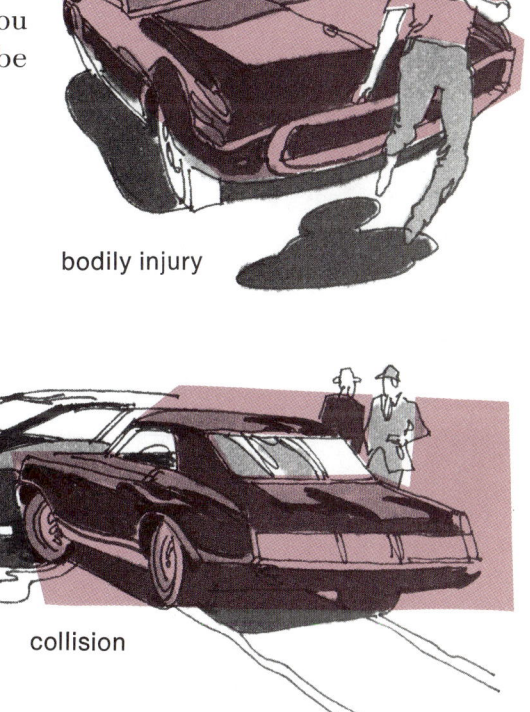

bodily injury

property damage

collision

taken to court. If you are found at fault, you must pay damages. You may have to pay many thousands of dollars. If you have bodily injury liability insurance, your insurance will pay for you. It is very important to have this kind of insurance. In most states, the law says you *must* have this kind of insurance.

2. **Property Damage Liability Insurance** The second kind of liability insurance is called *property damage* liability insurance. If you damage someone's property with your car, you can be taken to court. Again, if you are found at fault, you must pay damages. If you have property damage liability insurance, your insurance company will pay for you. In most states, the law says you *must* have this kind of insurance, too.

   Bodily injury and property damage liability insurance are both very important. If you do not have enough money to pay for liability insurance, don't buy a car. Driving without liability insurance is a foolish thing to do.

3. **Collision Insurance** Collision insurance pays for damage to your car if you run into something. Most of the time, you have to pay part of the cost yourself. You may have to pay for the first $50 or $100 damage. The insurance company pays the rest.

4. **Uninsured Motorist Insurance** Even though most states say that drivers — motorists — must have insurance, some do not. Suppose you are hurt by a driver who has no insurance. The law says he must pay the bills. But he may not have any money. It may take years to get the money if you get it at all. But if you have uninsured motorist insurance, you will be covered. Your

insurance company will pay for the damages. Uninsured motorist insurance will also pay the bills if you are hurt by a hit-and-run driver.

5. **Comprehensive Insurance** Your car may be damaged by things other than accidents. A tree may fall on it while it is parked. Someone may break one of the windows with a stone. The car may catch on fire. Comprehensive insurance pays for this kind of damage. It also pays if someone steals your car.

6. **Medical Costs Insurance** This kind of insurance pays the medical bills for anyone hurt while in your car. It covers you and your passengers, too.

There are other kinds of insurance besides these six kinds. Another kind of insurance will pay you money if you are hurt in an accident. Suppose you are hurt and can not work for a long time. This kind of insurance will pay you money until you can work again.

Not everyone needs the same kind of automobile insurance. Your insurance man will help you to pick the insurance that is right for you.

Buying Insurance

Not everyone needs the same kind of insurance. What kind of insurance should you have? How much insurance should you have? Talk it over with someone who sells automobile insurance. He will help you get the right kind. He will also tell you how much you must pay for your insurance.

Some people have to pay more for insurance than others. Men under 25 have to pay more for insurance. This is because these drivers have more accidents than other drivers. People who have had Driver Education do not pay as much. If you drive the family car, you do not pay as much. You have to pay much more if you have your own car.

Checking What You Have Read

1. Suppose you are in an accident. There is damage, but no one is hurt. What information does the law say you must give the other driver?
2. Suppose you have an accident at night. What can you do to warn other drivers there has been an accident?
3. Most of the time, it is better not to move a person who has been hurt. Why?
4. What kind of information do you need to fill out an accident report? Give three examples.
5. What are the two kinds of liability insurance?
6. What could happen if you have an accident and do not have liability insurance?
7. What is collision insurance? What does it cover?
8. If you have collision insurance, does the insurance company pay for *all* the damage?
9. Suppose a tree falls on your car. What kind of insurance would pay for the damage?

10. What is medical costs insurance? What does it cover?

11. What kind of insurance should *all* drivers have?

12. Why do men under 25 have to pay more for insurance?

To Talk About

1. Suppose you are driving at night. Another car runs into the side of your car. You are not hurt. The other driver is not hurt. But your passenger has a bad cut on his arm. Your car is damaged and you can not move it off the road. What would be the first thing you should do? What other things should you do after that?

2. Some people have to pay more for automobile insurance than others. Do you think this is right? Or do you think all drivers should pay the same for insurance?

3. Suppose a man saves his money to buy a car. He has just enough money to pay for the car and to run it. He does not have enough money to buy liability insurance. Is it all right for him to drive without insurance?

Things To Do

Find out about 'no fault' automobile insurance. You may live in a state that has 'no fault' insurance. Or your state may be about to change over to a 'no fault' plan. In what ways can 'no fault' insurance save drivers time and money? Are there still some problems about 'no fault' insurance to be worked out? Write a short report on what you find out.

CHAPTER 6

How a Car Works

"What a place to have car trouble!" said Mr. Kozak, shaking his head.

"What do we do now?" asked Mrs. Kozak.

"I don't know."

They had been driving on a back road. The car hit a large bump, and the engine stopped running. Mr. Kozak had tried to start it again and again. But nothing happened. They were miles from any town and had not seen another car for some time. At last, Mr. Kozak said, "I guess I'll have to fix it myself."

He got out of the car to look at the engine. So many parts! So many different *things*! Mr. Kozak knew nothing about automobiles, and never had. Someone else had always fixed his car for him when there was trouble. But now he would have to do it himself. He looked at one thing and then another. But he was not even sure what most of the parts were. After looking at the engine a long time, he got back in the car.

"Did you find the trouble?" asked Mrs. Kozak.

"No," he said. "I did not know what to look for. And even if I did, I don't have any tools to fix it with."

Just then, Mrs. Kozak saw another car coming. She started waving. The driver saw her and pulled off the road. He got out of his car and walked over. "Having trouble?" he asked.

"Yes," said Mr. Kozak. He told the man about how the engine had stopped running.

"Let me take a look," the man said. "I think I know what happened." After looking at the engine for a minute, he did something with his hand.

"Try it now," the man said.

The engine started at once. "What did you do?" Mr. Kozak asked. "How did you find the trouble so fast?"

"It was not hard," the man said. "The wire from your distributor had come out. It must have come out when you hit that bump. That sort of thing happens now and then. But it is fixed now." The man started walking back to his car.

"Thank you very much," Mr. Kozak said. "I don't know what we would have done if you had not come along."

"Glad to be of help," the man called.

Mr. Kozak pulled back on the road. "I saw that wire myself," he said. "But I did not know what it was for. Tomorrow, I'm going to start learning more about how a car works."

"Better late than never," said Mrs. Kozak, smiling.

Meet the Automobile

Most drivers know a little more about cars than Mr. Kozak. But few drivers have the skill needed to fix their own automobiles. Today's cars have just too many parts. It takes a lot of skill—as well as tools—to fix a car.

88

But a driver should know something about how a car works. He should know what the different parts are for. Knowing about your car can save you time and money. Suppose something goes wrong. If the trouble is small, you might be able to fix it yourself. Mr. Kozak could have fixed his car if he had known what to do.

By knowing how a car works you can also spot trouble-in-the-making. You may not be able to fix it yourself. But by spotting trouble early, you can get it fixed before the trouble gets bigger. This will save you money.

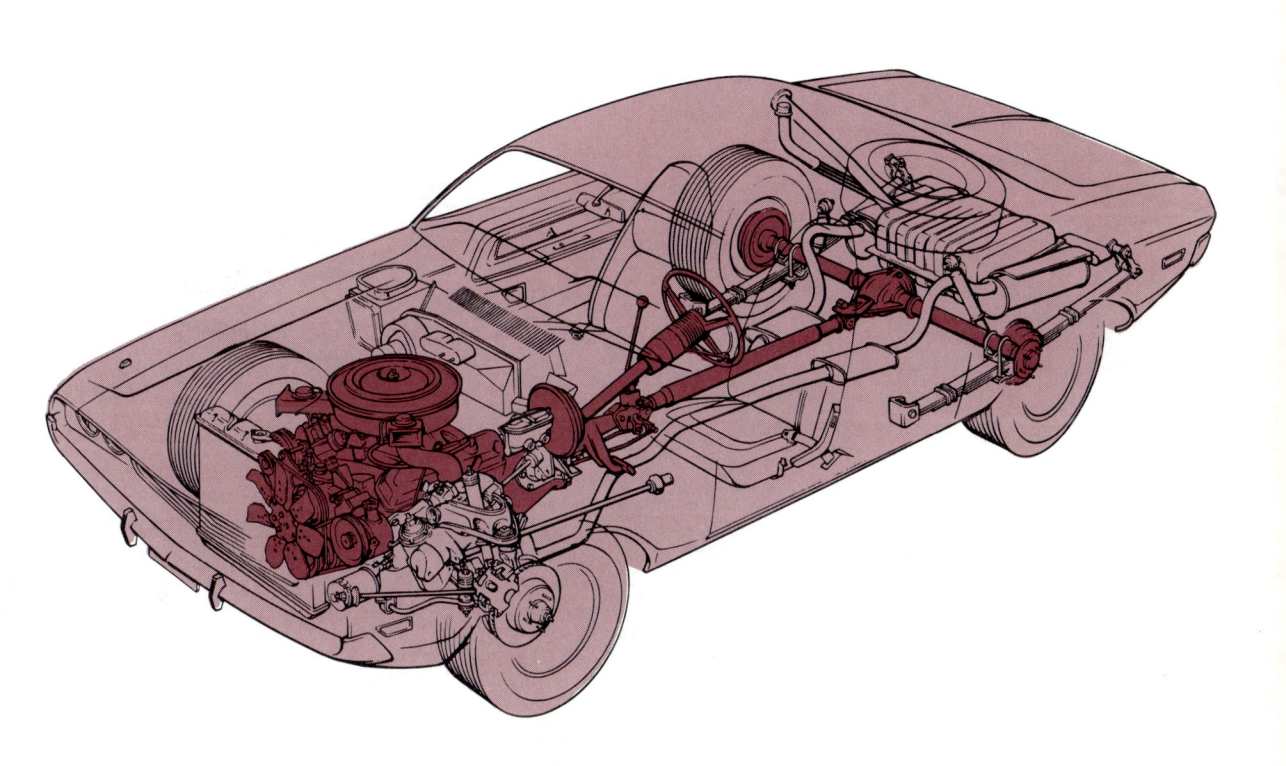

The Engine

The Fuel System

The engine needs gasoline and air to run. The fuel pump brings the gasoline from the gas tank to the carburetor. A filter cleans the gasoline before it gets to the carburetor. In the carburetor, the gasoline is mixed with air. This mix of gas and air then goes into the engine.

The air cleaner cleans the air before it gets to the carburetor. This keeps dirt from getting into the engine. There is a filter in the air cleaner. When

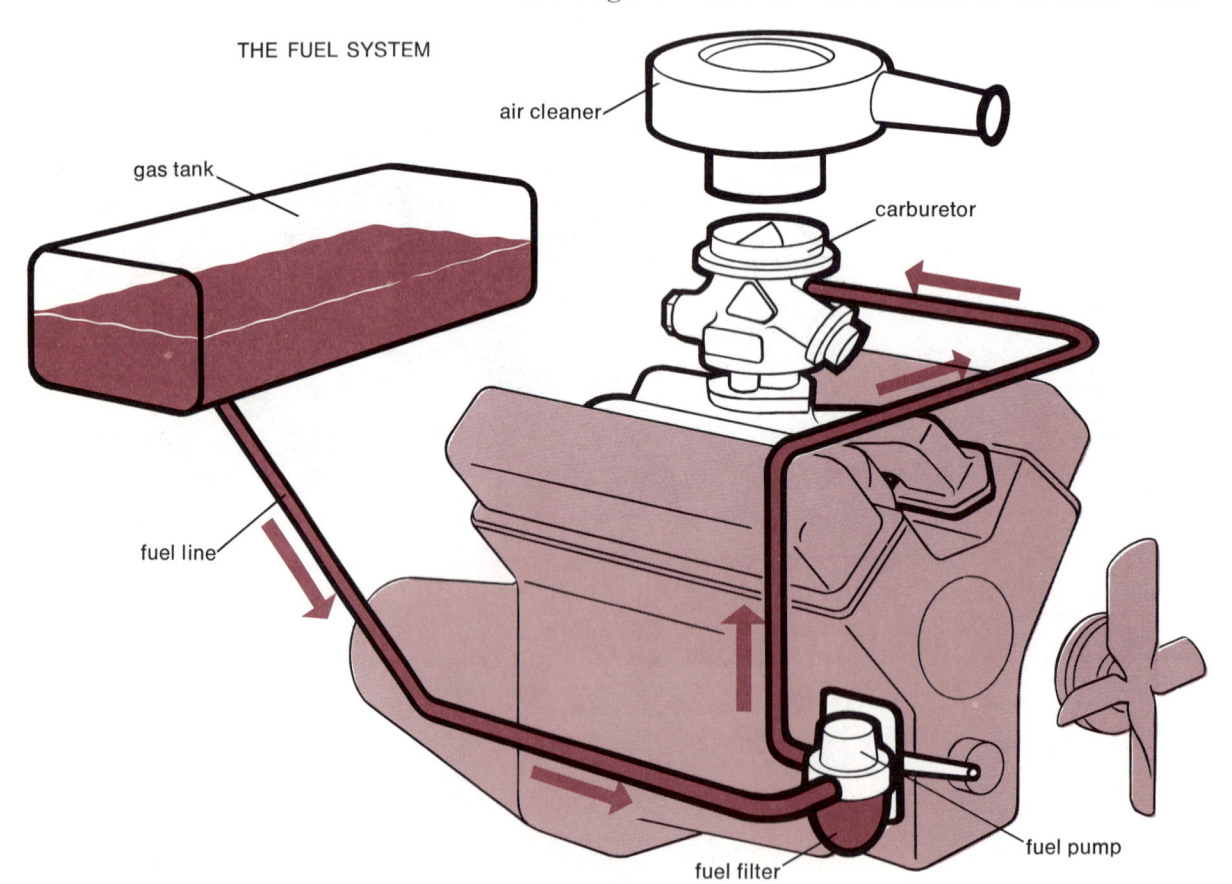

THE FUEL SYSTEM

gas tank

air cleaner

carburetor

fuel line

fuel filter

fuel pump

this filter gets dirty, it must be cleaned. From time to time, a new filter must be put in. You can do this yourself. It is not hard to do.

The Electrical System

The engine also needs electricity to run. Without electricity, the engine could not start. The alternator makes the electricity. The battery stores it. The distributor sends the electricity to the spark plugs at the right time. Wires carry electricity to other parts of the car that need it. The alternator and the battery work together to make and store this electricity.

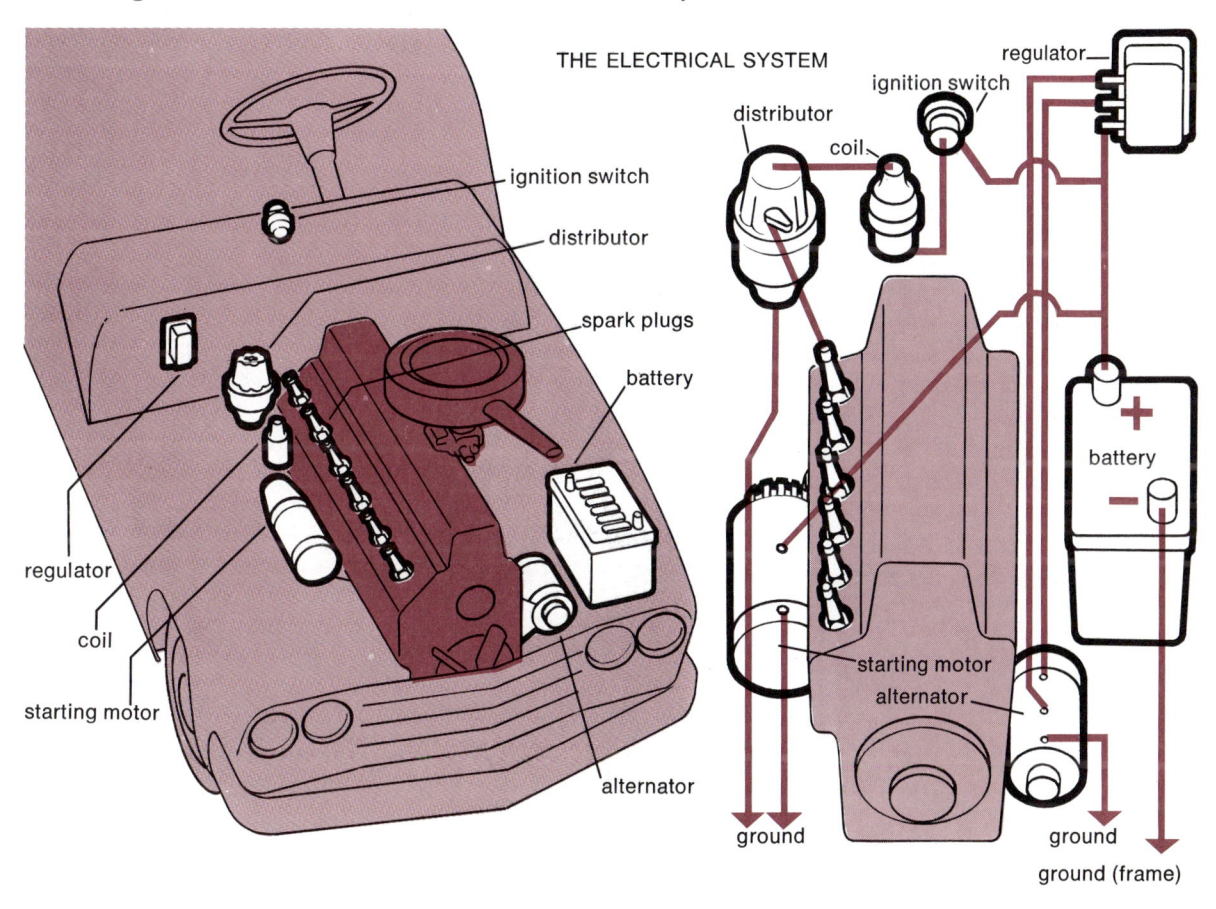

THE ELECTRICAL SYSTEM

REAR WHEEL DRIVE

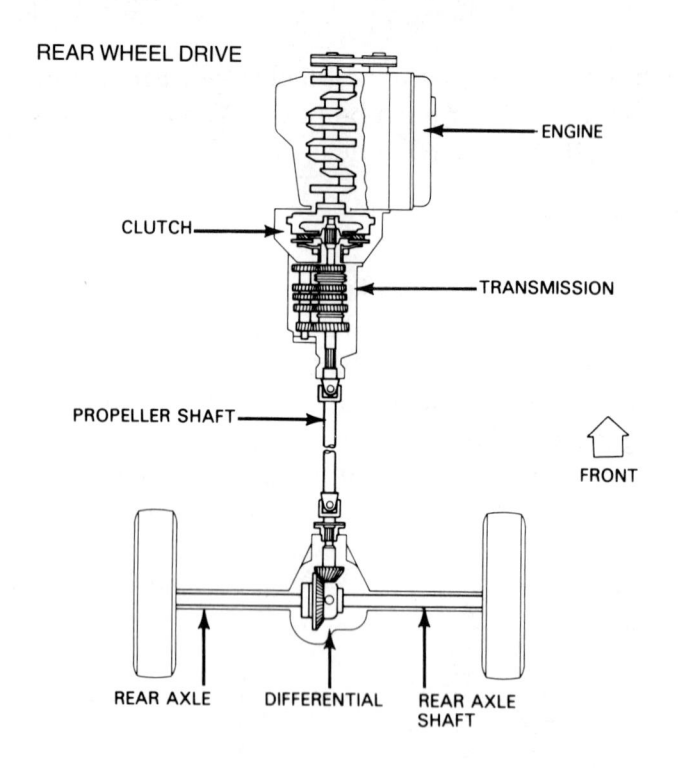

- ENGINE
- CLUTCH
- TRANSMISSION
- PROPELLER SHAFT
- FRONT
- REAR AXLE
- DIFFERENTIAL
- REAR AXLE SHAFT

FRONT WHEEL DRIVE

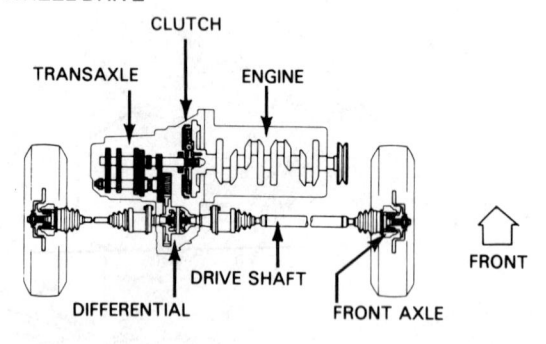

- CLUTCH
- TRANSAXLE
- ENGINE
- DRIVE SHAFT
- DIFFERENTIAL
- FRONT AXLE
- FRONT

The parts carrying power to the drive wheels are called the power train. The crankshaft is the first part of the power train. The crankshaft ends in a large metal plate called the flywheel. Another metal plate called the clutch presses against the

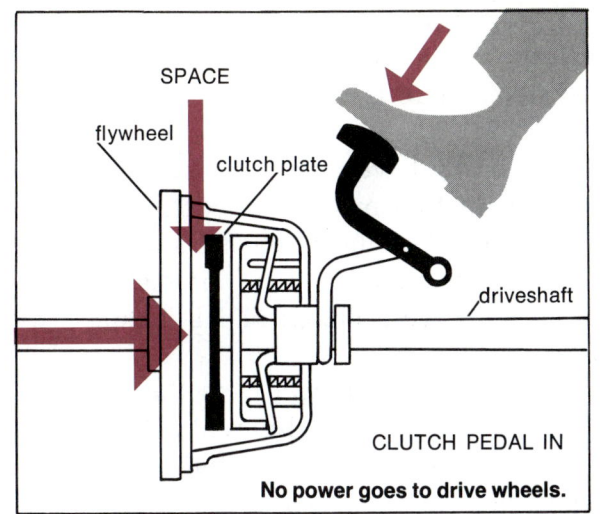

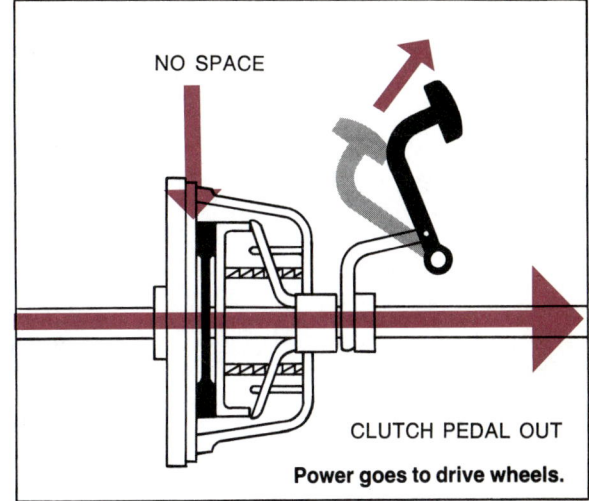

SPACE · flywheel · clutch plate · driveshaft
CLUTCH PEDAL IN
No power goes to drive wheels.

NO SPACE
CLUTCH PEDAL OUT
Power goes to drive wheels.

flywheel, carrying power to the transmission. When the driver pushes the clutch pedal in, the clutch pulls away from the flywheel. No power gets to the transmission. When he takes his foot off the pedal, the clutch presses against the flywheel again.

Behind the clutch is the transmission. The transmission is a set of gears. First gear is used to get

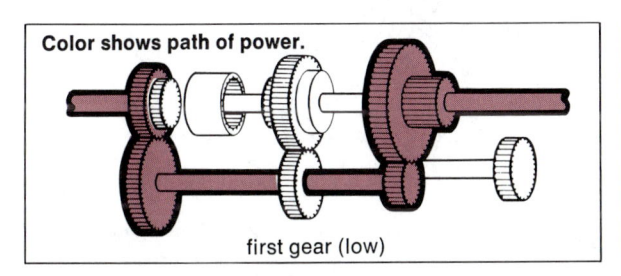

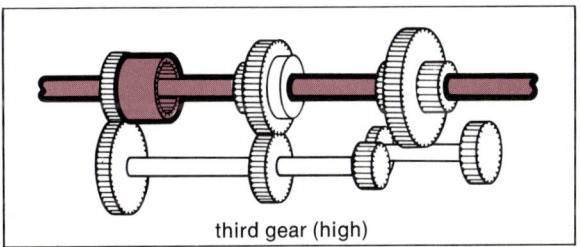

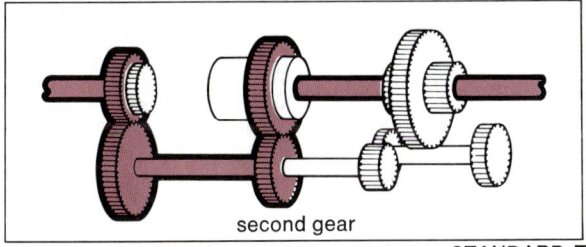

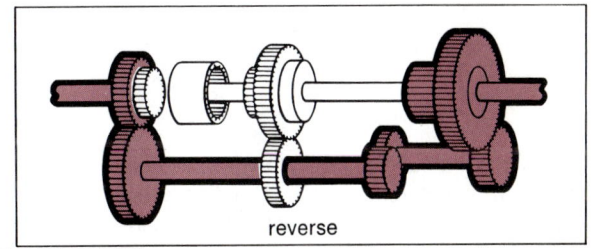

Color shows path of power.
first gear (low)

third gear (high)

second gear

reverse

STANDARD TRANSMISSION

the car moving. Second gear is used to make the car go a little faster. And third gear (high gear) is used after that. There is also a reverse gear so the car can back up.

Many cars today have automatic transmissions. With an automatic transmission, the driver does not have to shift gears. The automatic transmission shifts gears by itself. Cars with automatic transmissions do not have a clutch pedal. There is no need for one.

The driveshaft carries power from the transmission to the differential. The differential is another set of gears. One part of the differential sends power to the right axle. The other part sends power to the left axle. The axles then turn the drive wheels.

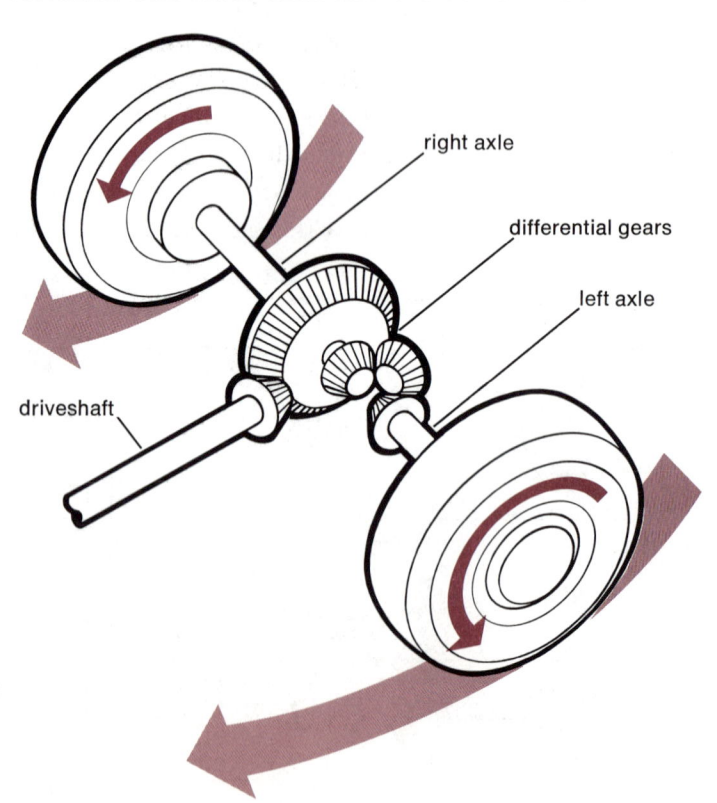

When going around a corner, the drive wheels must turn at different speeds. The differential lets the outside wheel turn faster than the inside wheel.

The Steering System

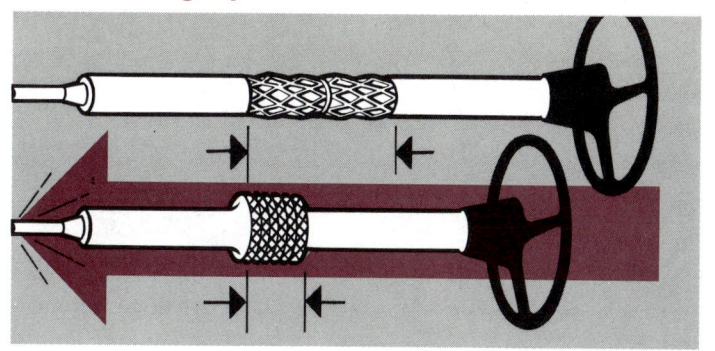

The steering column in today's cars is made for safety. If the car should run into something, the column gives way. It pushes in on itself. This keeps the driver from getting hurt so easily in an accident.

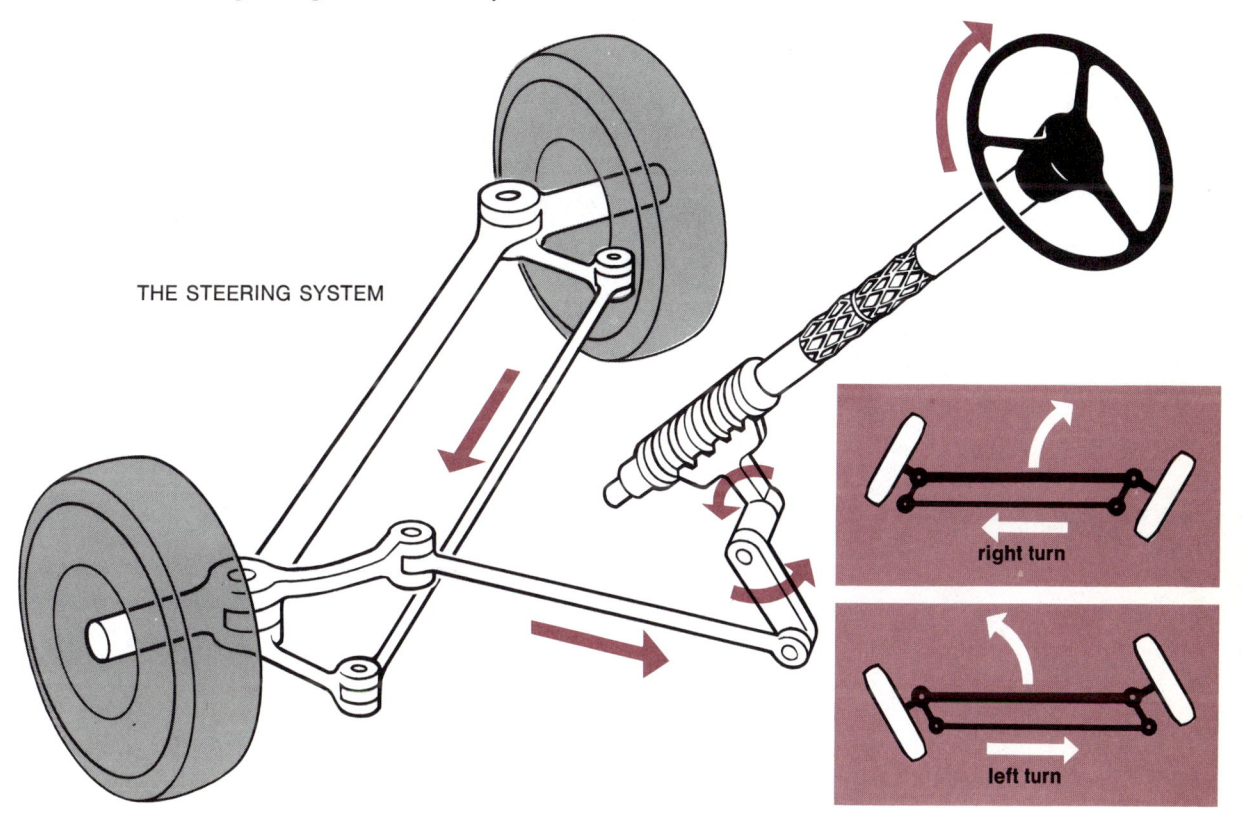

THE STEERING SYSTEM

right turn

left turn

disc

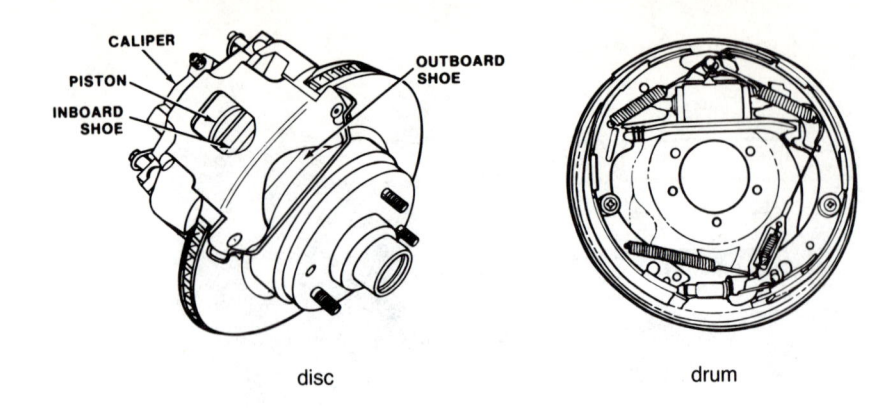

drum

Disc brakes are used on the front wheels. Drum brakes are usually used on the rear. Some expensive cars have disc brakes on the rear. The disc brake stops the car by clamping both sides of the discs that are attached to each wheel. The drum brake has shoes that expand against the drums attached to each rear wheel. If the driver pushes too hard on the brake pedal, he may stop the wheels from moving and cause a skid.

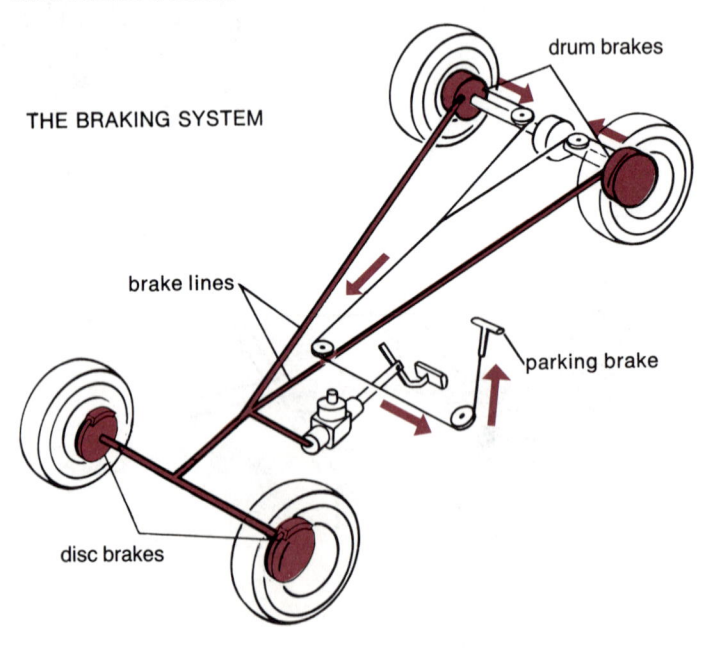

THE BRAKING SYSTEM

The Lubricating System

There are many moving parts in an automobile engine. The parts rub together, making friction. Friction always makes heat and wear. Oil between the moving parts cuts down on friction. Oil keeps the parts from wearing out or getting too hot from friction.

The oil is kept in a pan under the engine. The oil pump pushes oil to the moving parts in the engine. The oil filter keeps the oil clean. When the filter gets dirty, a new one must be put in. The oil must be changed from time to time, too.

Always make sure you have enough oil in your engine. The dipstick shows how much oil there is. By looking at the dipstick, you can tell when you need to put in more oil.

There are other moving parts outside the engine. These parts must also be lubricated from time to time. You can have this done at a service station.

THE LUBRICATING SYSTEM

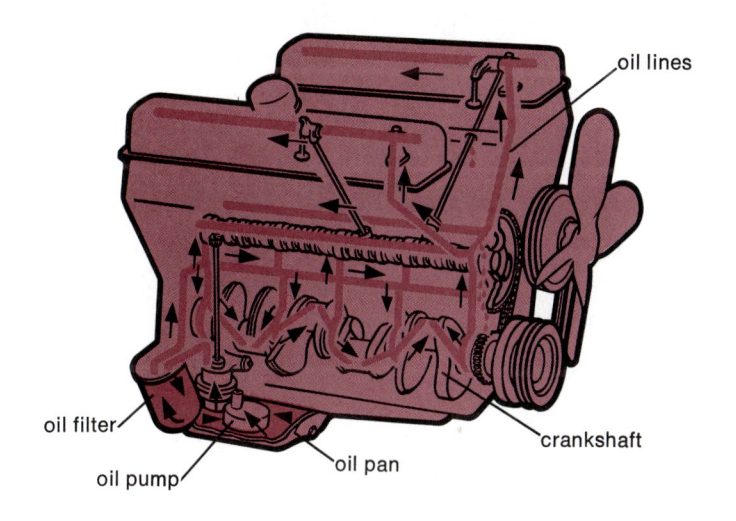

The Cooling System

THE COOLING SYSTEM

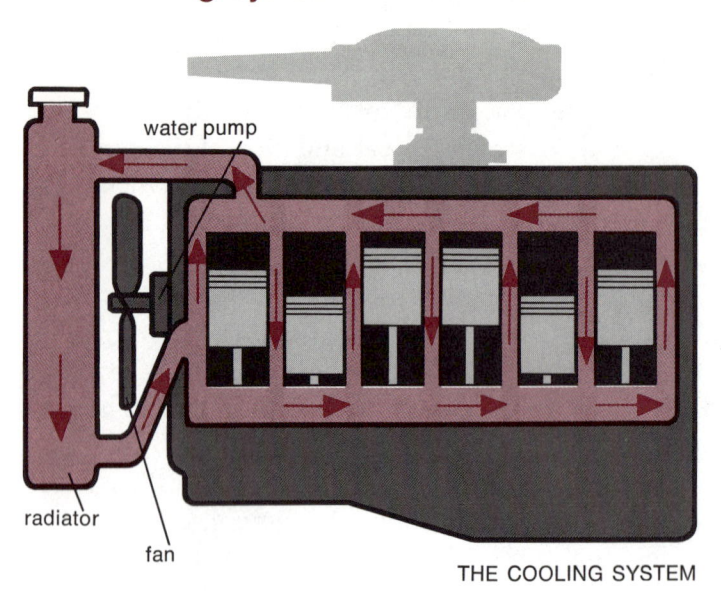

(Labels: water pump, radiator, fan)

The cooling system keeps the engine from getting too hot. Most cars use antifreeze and water in their cooling systems, even in the summer. A water pump pushes the hot coolant from the engine to the radiator. The fan cools the radiator. Then the coolant goes back into the engine. When the engine is cold, remove the radiator cap to see if the engine needs coolant. Never remove the radiator cap when the engine is warm.

Checking What You Have Read

1. Name the important parts in the fuel system of an automobile. Tell how gasoline gets to the carburetor.
2. What is an air cleaner? Where in the engine would you find it?
3. What should you do when the filter in the air cleaner gets dirty?

4. How does the carburetor work? What does it do?
5. Name the important parts in the electrical system. Tell how the electrical system is used to start the car.
6. In what way do the battery and the alternator work together? Why are *both* needed?
7. What does the transmission do? Why must a car have more than one gear?
8. Why is oil needed in the engine?
9. What does the water pump do?

To Talk About _____

Knowing how a car works is not important. If something goes wrong, you can always get someone to fix it for you. Do you agree with this? How much do you think a driver should know about automobiles?

Things To Do _____

By and large, most cars work the same way. All have engines, transmissions, brakes, and so on. But not all engines are the same. Some cars (and many trucks) have diesel engines. Find out about diesel engines. How are they different from other engines? In what ways are they better? Find out about rotary (Wankel) engines. How do rotary engines work? How are they different from other engines? Also look into turbine engines. Do you think cars may one day have turbine engines? Draw charts showing how these four kinds of engines work. Be ready to answer questions others in class may have.

CHAPTER 7

Inside the Car

You are now about to take the wheel for the first time. But before you start the engine, make sure you know your car inside and out. Learn where each indicator and control is. The indicators and controls are not in the same places on all cars. On the road, you will have no time to look for these things. You must know where they are *before* you start driving.

Indicators

Speedometer and Odometer

The speedometer tells how fast the car is going in miles per hour (mph). When driving in town, look at the speedometer often. Speed limits change. In

A driver must know where each control and indicator is. He should know where they are even without looking.

one part of town the speed limit may be 40 mph. In another part of town the speed limit may be 25 mph.

On the highway, you may not have to look at the speedometer as often. But watch your speed. Today's cars are quiet even at high speed. You may find yourself going faster than you think you are. Only by looking at the speedometer can you tell how fast you are going.

The odometer tells how many miles the car has gone. The odometer can help you when you are on a trip. It can also help you in taking care of your car. In some older cars, the oil should be changed every 1,000 miles. Most cars today need a change of oil only every 4,000 to 6,000 miles. The odometer will tell you when you have gone that far.

Alternator Warning Light and Ammeter

When the engine is running, the alternator generates electricity to operate the car. The alternator also charges the battery. If the alternator is not charging, the red alternator warning light comes on. If the car has an ammeter, it will read discharge when the alternator is not working.

If the alternator is not working, the car will stop when the battery is dead. If the warning light is on or the ammeter shows discharge when the engine is running, the car should be checked by a trained mechanic.

Oil Pressure Warning Light or Gauge

An oil pressure warning light will glow red if something is wrong. An oil pressure gauge will read very low if something is wrong. It may mean that the engine oil is dangerously low. Or there may be something broken or worn in the engine. The light does not tell the driver when to add oil. It tells only about the oil pressure. If the oil pressure is low the engine may wear out quickly.

When the oil pressure warning light comes on or the gauge reads low, pull over and stop the engine. If you keep driving, you may damage the engine. Use the dipstick to see if the oil is low. Add oil if needed. If the light or gauge still shows trouble after adding oil, call for a towtruck. Do not drive the car.

Temperature Gauge

The C on the temperature gauge stands for "cold." The H stands for "hot." When you first start the engine, the indicator is at the C. As the engine warms up, the indicator moves to the middle of the temperature gauge. The engine is then at its normal running temperature.

But if the indicator keeps moving until it gets to the H, something is wrong. The water in the engine is too hot. It is not cooling the engine as it should.

Trouble	What Might Be Wrong
engine too hot	slipping fan belt broken fan belt leak in radiator leak in radiator hose
alternator warning light comes on	slipping fan belt broken fan belt alternator worn out battery worn out
oil pressure warning light comes on	leak in oil hose leak in oil filter leak in oil pan oil pump worn out

If this happens when you are driving, do not stop right away. If you do, the water temperature will go up even more. When you turn off the engine, the water pump and fan stop working. Try to get to a gas station before you stop.

If you can not get to a gas station, you may have to stop. Try to find out what is wrong. But do not open the radiator cap right away. The hot water will come blowing out and burn you. Let the water cool before you open the radiator. Then start the engine again and put more water into the radiator. Put the water in a little at a time. Too much cold water all at once could crack the engine.

Fuel Gauge

The fuel gauge tells how much gas there is in the gas tank. The F on the gauge stands for 'full.' The E stands for 'empty.' When the indicator gets near the E, it is time to buy more gas.

Controls for Safety

Seat Lever

Some drivers are short. Some are tall. The seat lever lets the front seat be moved to suit the driver. Before you drive, make sure the seat is in the right place for you.

Seat Belts and Air Bags

Both the driver and his passengers should fasten their belts. If you are in an accident without your belt, you may be hurt. Some cars also have air bags. If the car hits something, air bags expand in front of you and keep your body from hitting the dash. Air bags protect you only in a head-on collision. You must wear a seat and shoulder belt for complete protection.

Rearview Mirrors

When you drive, you must see what is ahead. But you must also know what is behind you or to the side. It is dangerous to turn your head around to look. This is why the two rearview mirrors are so important. They help you to know if it is safe to stop, turn, or change lanes.

Light Controls

On most cars, the control for the headlights is to the left of the steering wheel. Pulling the control out part way turns on the parking lights. Pulling it out all the way turns on the headlights. On many cars, this control is also used to dim the indicator and gauge lights. Turning the control to the left makes them dim.

The headlights have two settings—high beam and low beam. A dimmer switch on the floor con-

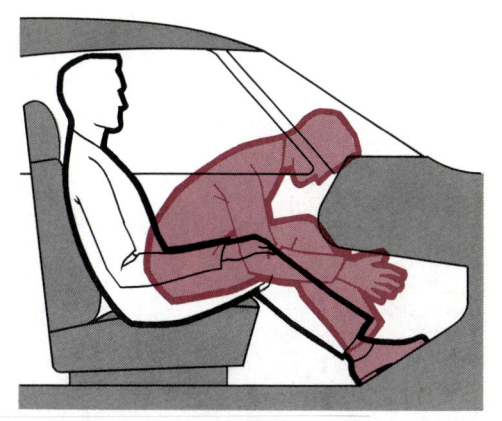

NO BELT

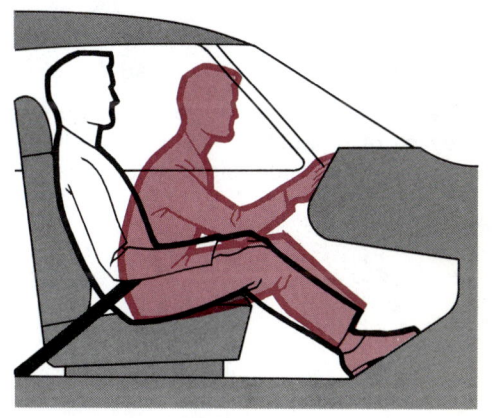

LAP BELT ONLY

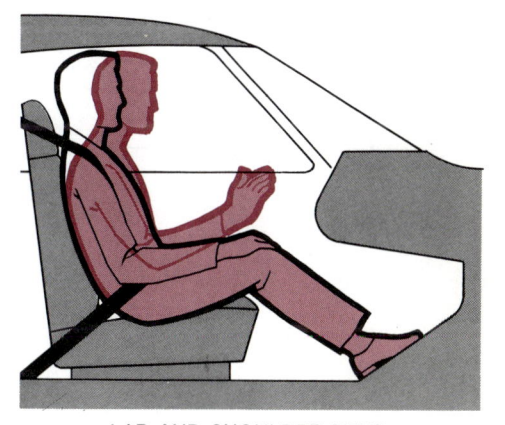

LAP AND SHOULDER BELT

with inside mirror only

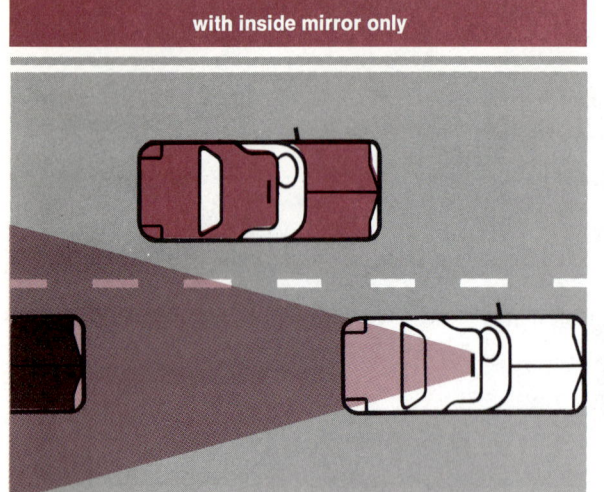

with both rearview mirrors

The outside rearview mirror helps a driver see more of what is behind him. Always check your outside mirror before passing or changing lanes.

trols the settings. Push the dimmer switch with your left foot to change from high to low beam. When the high beam is on, a small red indicator light also goes on. This indicator light, in or near the speedometer, tells you the high beam is on.

When the headlights or parking lights are turned on, the tail lights also go on. The brake lights go on when the driver pushes on the brake. Back-up lights go on when the car is put into reverse gear. Like the brake lights, the back-up lights work if the headlights are on or not. Back-up lights help the driver to see what is behind him at night. They also warn other drivers that the car is backing up.

Windshield Wipers and Washers

The control for the windshield wipers is next to the control for the headlights. The windshield wipers have two speeds. Cars today also have windshield washers. On many cars, the control for the wipers also controls the washers. If mud splashes on your windshield, you can clean it off at once. Windshield washers help you to see clearly.

Defroster and Heater

On cold days, the defroster keeps the windshield clear. Warm air blowing up from the bottom of the windshield takes off frost and ice. On winter days, the heater will keep the car warm. But even on very cold days, keep one window open a little. There is always a danger of carbon monoxide when the car is closed up.

Sun Visors

Over the windshield are the sun visors. There is one for the driver and one for the front seat passenger. If the sun gets in your eyes, you can pull the sun visor down. You can push it to one side if the sun is coming from the left.

Horn

Most cars have a horn control inside the steering wheel. The driver presses on this control to sound the horn. The horn should be used only to signal or to sound a warning. It should not be used to try to make others get out of your way.

Turn Signals

The control for the turn signals is on the left side of the steering column. When you are planning to turn right, you push it up. When you are planning to turn left, you push it down. After you have made the turn, the turn signal will go off by itself. But sometimes you must turn the signal off by hand. Suppose you signal that you are going to change lanes. You do not turn enough for the signal to go off by itself. You must turn it off yourself.

Green indicator lights show when your turn signals are on. There is one light for the left signal and another for the right signal. Sometimes you may not know if a turn signal is on or not. Check the indicator lights to find out.

Emergency Flashers

Emergency flashers are an important safety feature. A driver can turn them on if he has to stop because of trouble. When the emergency flasher control is turned on, all four turn signal lights start flashing. This warns other drivers that there is a stopped car ahead.

Driving Controls

Ignition Switch

The ignition switch has three positions. The first position is used to lock the car. The second position is used to start the car. The driver turns the key to the right and holds it there. At the same time, he presses down a little on the accelerator. As soon as

In a standard transmission car, the clutch pedal is always to the left of the brake pedal. The accelerator is to the right of the brake pedal. The dimmer switch, on the far left, controls the high-beam headlights. To change from low beam to high beam, tap the switch with your foot. To change back, tap the switch a second time.

the engine starts, he lets go of the key. The third position is used to play the radio when the engine is not running.

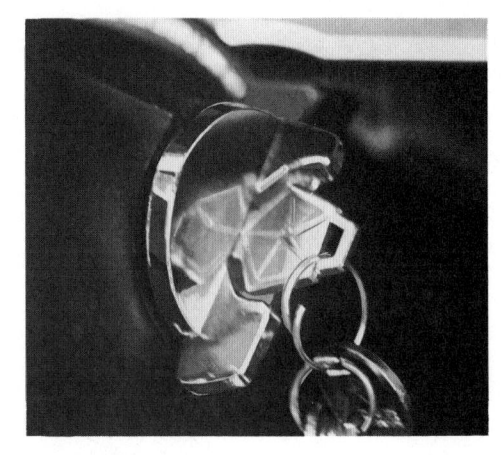

Steering Wheel

As you know, the steering wheel is used to make the car turn. If the steering wheel is turned to the right, the car turns right. If it is turned to the left, the car turns left. When you are backing up, the steering wheel works the same way. The direction you turn the wheel is the direction the car will go. Some cars have power steering. On these cars it is very easy to turn the wheel.

When the key is in Lock position, the steering wheel can not be turned.

Accelerator

The driver operates the accelerator with his right foot. The more he presses down on the pedal, the more gas the engine gets. The more gas the engine gets, the faster the car goes.

Brake Pedal

The brake pedal is next to the accelerator. The driver uses his right foot to slow or stop the car. Pushing on the brake pedal operates all four brakes. Some cars have power brakes. With power brakes, the driver does not have to push so hard to stop. But the car does not stop any faster than a car without power brakes. It still takes as much distance to stop.

Parking Brake

The parking brake keeps the car from moving when it is parked. On some cars, the driver sets the parking brake with his hand. On other cars, he pushes a pedal to put the parking brake on. On many cars, an indicator light shows the driver when his parking brake is on.

Clutch Pedal

When the driver pushes in the clutch pedal, no power can get to the rear wheels. The driver pushes in the clutch pedal when starting the engine. He also pushes it in each time he changes gears. Cars with automatic transmissions do not have a clutch pedal.

Standard Gearshift Selector

This lever is used to change gears on cars that have a standard gearshift. The lever may be on the right side of the steering column. Or it may be on the floor of the car.

Automatic Transmission Selector

In many ways, this lever is like the standard gearshift lever. It is used to put the car in the right gear. But a driver with an automatic transmission does not have to change gears. The automatic transmission does that for him. All he has to do is pick the gear or set of gears he wants. The automatic transmission does the rest. Sometimes the automatic transmission selector is on the steering column. Sometimes it is on the floor.

The letters on the selector stand for the different gears.

> **P** means park
>
> **R** means reverse
>
> **N** means neutral
>
> **D** means drive
>
> **L** means low

We will say more about these different gears in the next part of the book.

In some cars the gear selector or gearshift lever is on the steering column. In others these controls are on the floor.

Learning Where Things Are

Before you begin driving, learn where each control is. Sit behind the wheel of the car you will drive. Where is the seat lever? How is the parking brake set? Is there an oil pressure gauge? Or is there just an indicator light? Try to find each control without looking. Close your eyes and try to picture where each indicator is. Keep at it until you know where everything is.

111

Checking What You Have Read

1. Why must a driver know where all the gauges are before he starts driving?

2. Why is the odometer an important indicator? Name two ways in which the odometer can help a driver.

3. Suppose the alternator warning light comes on when you are driving. What does this mean? What should you do?

4. What should you do if the oil pressure warning light comes on while you are driving?

5. How can you find out how much oil you have in your engine? Will the oil pressure warning light tell you?

6. What does the C on the temperature gauge stand for? What does the H stand for?

7. Suppose your temperature gauge shows that the engine is getting too hot. Should you stop right away? What should you do?

8. Why must water be added to the radiator slowly and only a little at a time?

9. What does the E on the fuel gauge stand for? What does the F stand for?

10. Suppose a driver is in an accident. What can happen if he is not wearing his seat belt?

11. Why are two rearview mirrors needed? Would one be enough?

12. Suppose you are driving at night. Your headlights are on low beam. How would you change to high beam? How would you change back to low beam again?

13. What indicator tells a driver his high beam headlights are on?

14. Do all cars have clutch pedals?

15. Why are windshield washers an important safety feature?
16. What does the defroster do?
17. How can you tell if one of your turn signals is on?
18. Can a car with power brakes stop faster than a car without power brakes?
19. At night, back-up lights help a driver to see what is behind him. But back-up lights are important in the daytime, too. Why?

To Talk About

1. On some cars, there are gauges to show oil pressure, engine temperature, and alternator condition. Other cars have only warning lights to tell about these things. Which do you think are better, gauges or lights? Why?
2. Now and then, you will spot a driver who "drives with his horn." He uses his horn to try to make others get out of his way. What kind of driving personality do you think a person like this has? Do you think such a person would be a good driver?

Things To Do

Talk with 10 or 12 licensed drivers. Ask each one about using seat belts. Does each driver always use his seat belt? Do some drivers use their seat belts only now and then? What reasons do they give for not using seat belts? Make a list of these reasons. Are *any* of these reasons good reasons? Why not? What do you think can be done to get more people to wear their seat belts? Suppose a car could not be started if the driver was not wearing his seat belt. Would this be a good way to get everyone to wear seat belts? Can you think of a better way? Write a short report telling what you would do.

CHAPTER **8**

Now It's Your Turn To Take the Wheel

The time you have been waiting for is here at last. You are about to take the wheel yourself.

First, make sure the seat is in the right place for you. Can you see over the steering wheel without trouble? Can you reach all the pedals easily? Use the seat lever to move the seat to suit you.

Now check both rearview mirrors. Move the inside mirror so that you can see all of the rear window. Move the outside mirror so that you can see behind and to the left. You should also be able to see part of the left side of your car.

Put on your seat belt. The belt should fit close but not too tight. Have your passengers put on their seat belts, too. Then make sure all the doors are locked. You are now ready to start the engine.

The Automatic Transmission Car

If your car has an automatic transmission, you do not have to shift gears. The automatic transmission will do that for you. But first you have to "tell" the transmission what you want it to do. This is done by moving the automatic transmission selector. On most cars, there are five positions.

N Neutral The engine is disconnected from the drive wheels. The wheels are not locked. The car can roll or be pushed, if the brakes are off.

D Drive Most driving is done in this position. When the transmission is put in drive, the car begins to move forward.

L Low Low is used to drive up or down steep hills. It is used when the car is pulling a heavy load. Low is also used when driving through mud or sand.

R Reverse This is the position used for backing the car. Never try to put the transmission in this position when the car is moving forward. You could ruin the transmission.

P Park The transmission should be put in this position when the engine is turned off. In park, the transmission is locked. The car will not move. It can not roll away. The engine can be started in the park position.

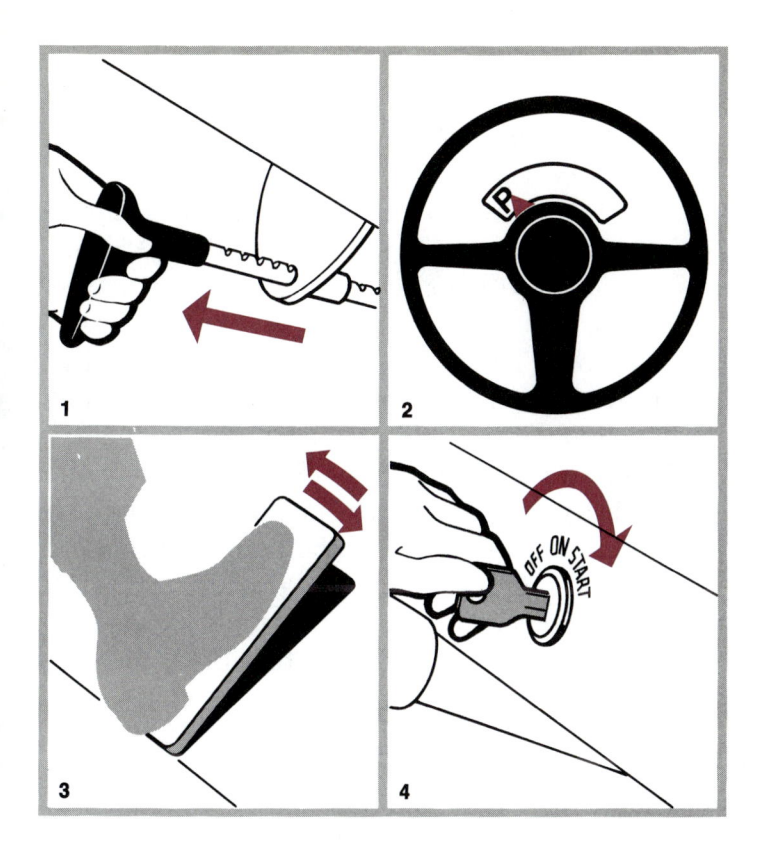

Starting the Engine

1. Be sure the parking brake is on before you start.
2. Put the transmission selector in the P (park) position.
3. If the engine is cold, push the accelerator to the floor once. Then release it.
4. Turn the ignition key all the way to the right and hold it there. At the same time, press down on the accelerator just a little.
5. Let go of the key as soon as the engine starts. Give the engine a minute or two to warm up.

The "9 and 3" Steering Position

Before you get under way, check your steering position. For best control, you should hold the wheel as shown here. Think of the steering wheel as the face of a clock. Place your left hand at the "9 o'clock" position. Place your right hand at the "3 o'clock" position.

Keep both hands on the wheel when you drive. Only when signalling or operating a control should you take one hand off the wheel.

Some cars have power steering. These cars turn very easily. Beginning drivers often find that these cars turn *too* easily. The beginning driver may have a hard time keeping the car under control. He will steer too much to the right or left. Power steering makes driving easier. But the driver must first get the "feel" of it.

1. After the engine has warmed up, you are ready to go forward. First, press down on the brake pedal with your right foot.
2. Then move the transmission selector to D.
3. Release the parking brake. But keep your foot on the brake pedal.
4. Check traffic by looking in both rearview mirrors. Then take a quick look all around to make sure it is safe to start.
5. Signal that you are about to start moving. Use a turn signal or a hand signal.
6. Take your foot off the brake and press very gently on the accelerator. The car will begin to move forward.

1

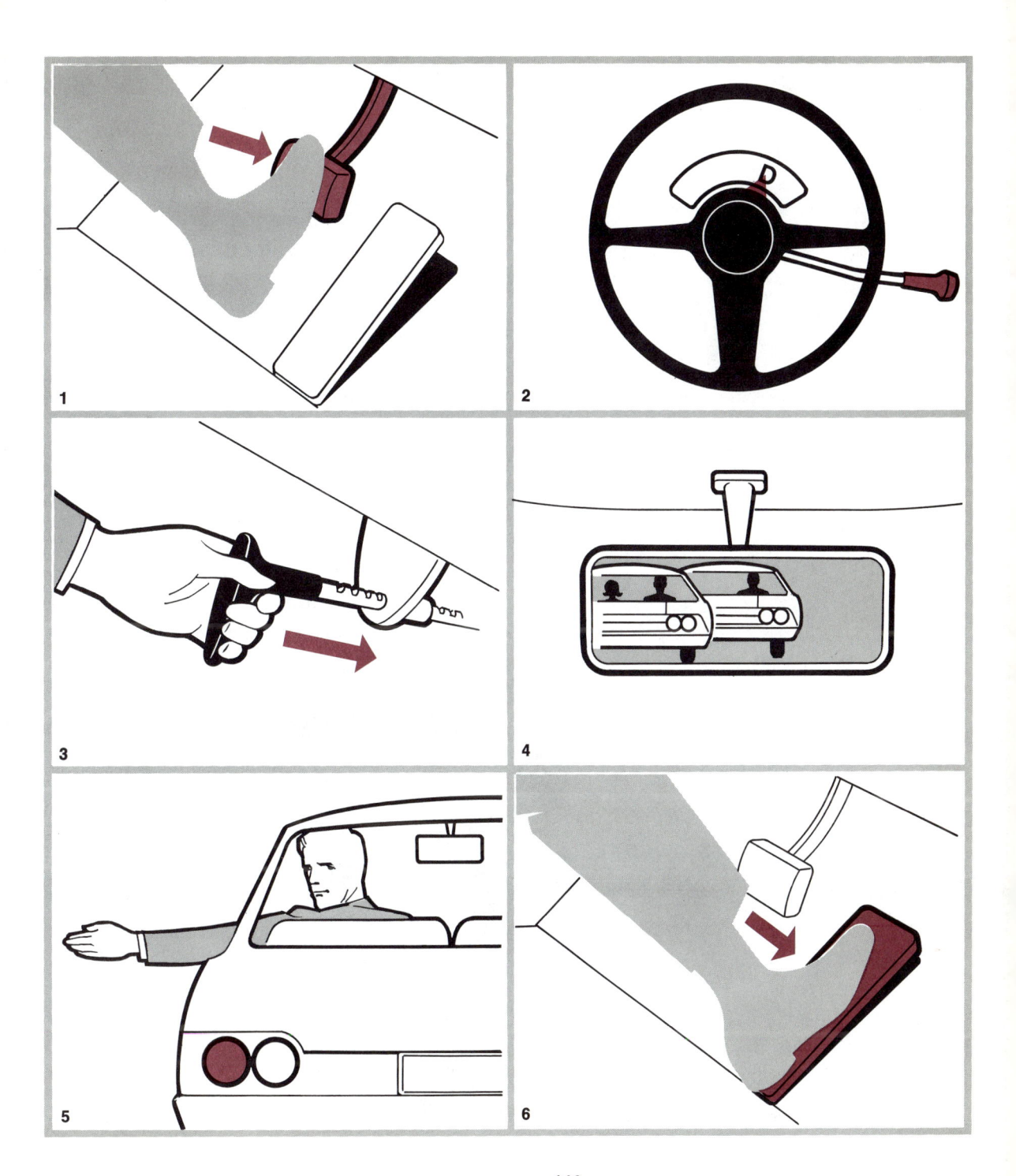

2

3

4

5

6

Stopping the Car

First, check the rearview mirrors to be sure it is safe to stop. Signal that you are stopping. Take your foot off the accelerator. Then press down gently on the brake pedal. Just before the car stops, let up a little on the brake. This will help bring the car to a smooth stop. For short stops, you can leave the car in D. But you must keep your foot on the brake. Cars with automatic transmissions "creep." The car moves slowly forward even when you don't have your foot on the accelerator. This is why you must keep your foot on the brake. For longer stops, put the car in N or P.

After parking the car, always put it in P. Set the parking brake. Then turn off the ignition. Keep your foot on the brake until you have turned off the ignition. Before you get out, roll up any open windows. When you leave, lock all doors. Never leave your key in the ignition or on the seat when you park.

Always signal before stopping. On bright days, the driver following you may not see your brake lights so easily. For added safety, also give a hand signal.

The Standard Transmission Car

Driving a car with a standard transmission takes more practice. There are more controls and more things to do. But it is also good to know how to drive a standard transmission car. This skill can be of great help in an emergency. But build up your driving skills in an automatic transmission car first. Then, if you wish, you can learn to operate a standard transmission car.

The gearshift lever on many standard transmission cars is on the steering column. On some cars it is on the floor. You shift gears by moving the lever to different positions.

Neutral When the car is in neutral, no power can get to the rear wheels.

First Gear This is the gear used to get the car moving from a stop. First gear is also used when driving up or down a *very* steep hill. A car has the most pulling power in first gear.

Second Gear At about 10 mph, the driver shifts from first to second gear. Second gear is used to get the car moving faster. It is also used when driving up or down some hills.

Third Gear (High Gear) At about 20 mph, the driver shifts from second gear to third gear. Third (high) gear is used for most driving.

Reverse Gear This is the gear used for backing.

Before you start the engine, learn where each gear position is. Practice shifting from one gear to another. Also practice using the clutch pedal. You must push it in each time you shift gears. You also push it in before starting the engine or stopping.

Starting the Engine

1. Be sure the parking brake is on.
2. Push the clutch pedal in all the way.
3. Check to see that the car is in neutral.
4. If the engine is cold, push the accelerator to the floor once. Then release it.
5. Turn the ignition key all the way to the right and hold it there. At the same time, press down on the accelerator just a little.
6. Let go of the key as soon as the engine starts. Also let up on the accelerator. Give the engine a minute or two to warm up.

Getting Under Way

1. Push the clutch pedal in with your left foot.
2. Shift to first gear. Keep the clutch pedal all the way in.
3. Release the parking brake.
4. Check the rearview mirrors to see if it is safe to pull out. Look around in all directions.
5. Signal that you are about to start moving. Use a turn signal or a hand signal.
6. Press gently on the accelerator and let the clutch out slowly. Let the clutch out until you reach the *friction point*. This is the point at which the car is about to move. Hold the clutch at the friction point for a second or two. Then slowly let it out the rest of the way. (If you let the clutch out too fast, the engine will stop.)
7. At about 10 mph, push in the clutch and let up on the accelerator. Shift to second gear. Slowly

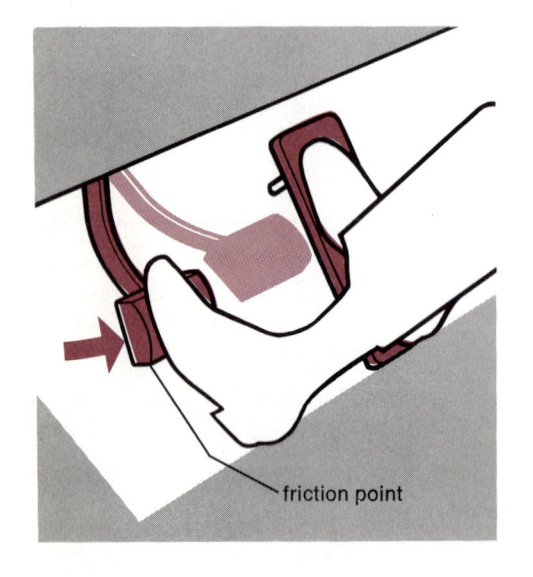

let out the clutch and press gently on the accelerator again.

8. At about 20 mph, shift to third gear. Follow the same steps you did in shifting to second gear. Push in the clutch and let up on the accelerator. Then move the gearshift to the third gear position. Let the clutch out slowly. At the same time, begin to press on the accelerator again.

Stopping the Car

After checking the rearview mirrors, signal that you are stopping. Take your foot off the accelerator. Press gently on the brake pedal with your right foot. When you have slowed to about 15 mph, push in the clutch pedal with your left foot. Keep the brakes on until the car stops. Then shift to neutral.

Sometimes you may have to stop while you are still in first gear. When this happens, put the clutch in at the same time you begin braking. If you don't, the engine may stop running.

Shifting Down

The engine has more pulling power in second or first than in high. When you slow down, you may have to shift from high to second. You have to shift down, for example, when you turn at an intersection. An automatic transmission shifts down by itself. With a standard transmission, you have to shift down yourself. When you slow to under 20 mph, always shift down to second gear. Also shift down to second gear when driving down a long or steep hill. Use your engine as a brake. This will keep you from going too fast. You will still need to use your brakes, but not as much.

Checking What You Have Read

1. List the five positions on an automatic transmission selector.
2. What five steps should you follow in starting the engine? List each step.
3. What is the "10 o'clock and 2 o'clock" steering position?
4. Most of the time, you should keep both hands on the wheel. When do you need to take one hand off the wheel? Give two examples.
5. If you stop for a short time, you can leave the car in D. But you must keep your foot on the brake. Why?
6. When driving an automatic transmission car, when should you use low gear? Give three examples.
7. When driving a standard transmission car, when should you shift down to a lower gear? Give three examples.
8. In a standard transmission, what is the "friction point"?

To Talk About

1. A driver's seating position is very important. But no car has ever been made that will "fit" every driver just right. Moving the seat lever can help. But often this is not enough. What else can a driver do to give himself a better seating position?
2. Driving an automatic transmission car is easier than driving a standard transmission car. But some people like standard transmission cars better. In what ways is a standard transmission better than an automatic transmission? In what ways is an automatic transmission better than a standard transmission?

Things To Do

Not all automatic transmissions have the same kind of selectors. In some cars, the selector is on the steering column. In others, it is on the floor. Many cars have more than one Low position. There may be a L-1 position and a L-2 position. Make a large chart showing the different kinds of transmission selectors. Use pictures cut from magazines, or make your own drawings. Then make another chart showing the different kinds of standard transmission gearshifts. Some cars have three forward gears. Others have as many as five forward gears. Show pictures of as many kinds of gearshifts as you can find. Be ready to answer any questions others in class may have.

CHAPTER 9

Turning, Backing, and Parking

You have now learned how to start a car and make it go forward. You have also learned how to bring it to a smooth stop. These are important skills. But there are still many other skills you must learn.

Next you will learn about turning, backing, and parking. These are skills you will need to know before you are ready to drive in traffic. But before you learn about these three skills, you must learn about another way of steering.

Hand-Over-Hand Steering

For most straight-ahead driving, you should steer with your hands in the "10 and 2" position. But when turning, you should use hand-over-hand steering. The pictures here show how hand-over-hand steering is used to turn right. To begin the turn, place your right hand near the top of the steering wheel. Start turning until that hand is near the "bottom" of the wheel. Let the steering wheel slide through your left hand. Then continue turning with the left hand. At the same time, bring your right hand back to the top of the wheel. To make a left turn, start with your left hand on top of the wheel.

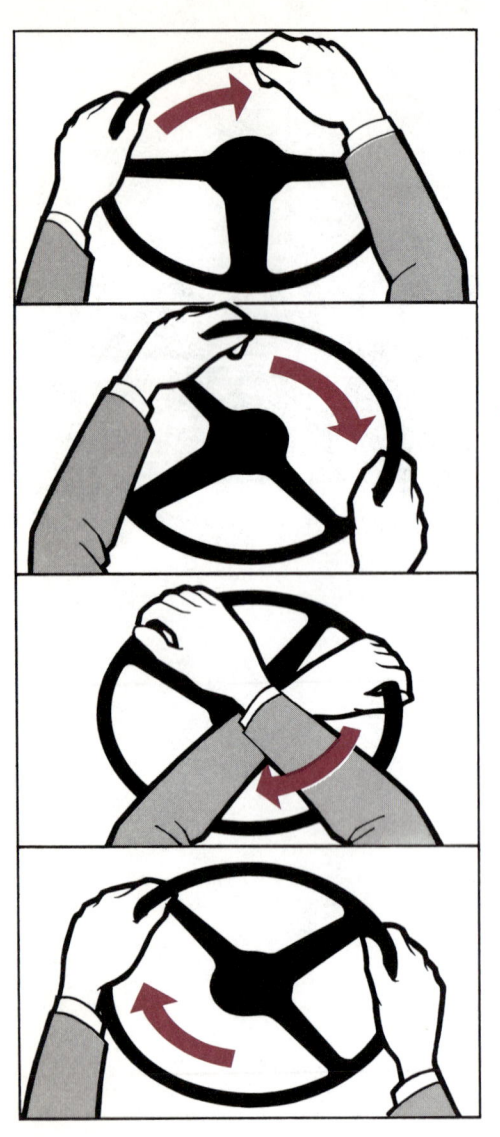

Turning

Always slow down before turning. If you are driving a standard transmission car, shift down to second. When turning right, your car should be about 3 feet from the curb.

Timing is important. Do not start your turn too soon or too late. If you start a right turn too soon, your rear wheel will hit the curb. When making a right turn you should end up in the right lane. If you start turning too late, you will end up in the left lane.

When turning left, you *should* end up in the left lane (the lane nearest the center line). Make sure it is safe before you start turning. While waiting to make a left turn, keep the front wheels straight. Do not turn in front of oncoming cars. Watch out for pedestrians in the crosswalk. You must yield the right-of-way to them.

Right Turn

1. Check traffic in all directions. Watch out for cars behind you and to the right.
2. Signal for a right turn.
3. Move into the right-hand lane if you are not already in it.

RIGHT TURN

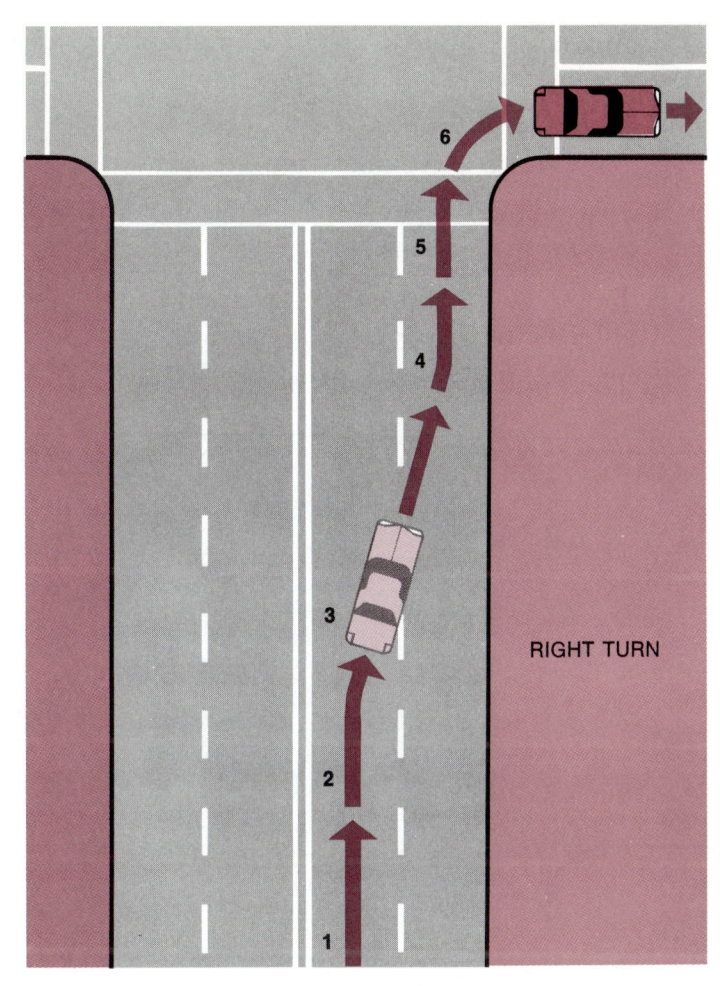

4. Slow down and signal again.
5. Just before turning, check traffic again. Watch out for pedestrians.
6. Begin your turn as the car moves into the intersection.

Left Turn

1. Check traffic in all directions. Watch out for cars behind you and to the left.
2. Signal for a left turn.

3. Move into the lane just to the right of the center line. On a one-way street, move to the lane on the far left.
4. Slow down and signal again.
5. Just before turning, check traffic again. Watch out for pedestrians.
6. Begin your turn as the car moves into the intersection.
7. Then pull into the right lane.

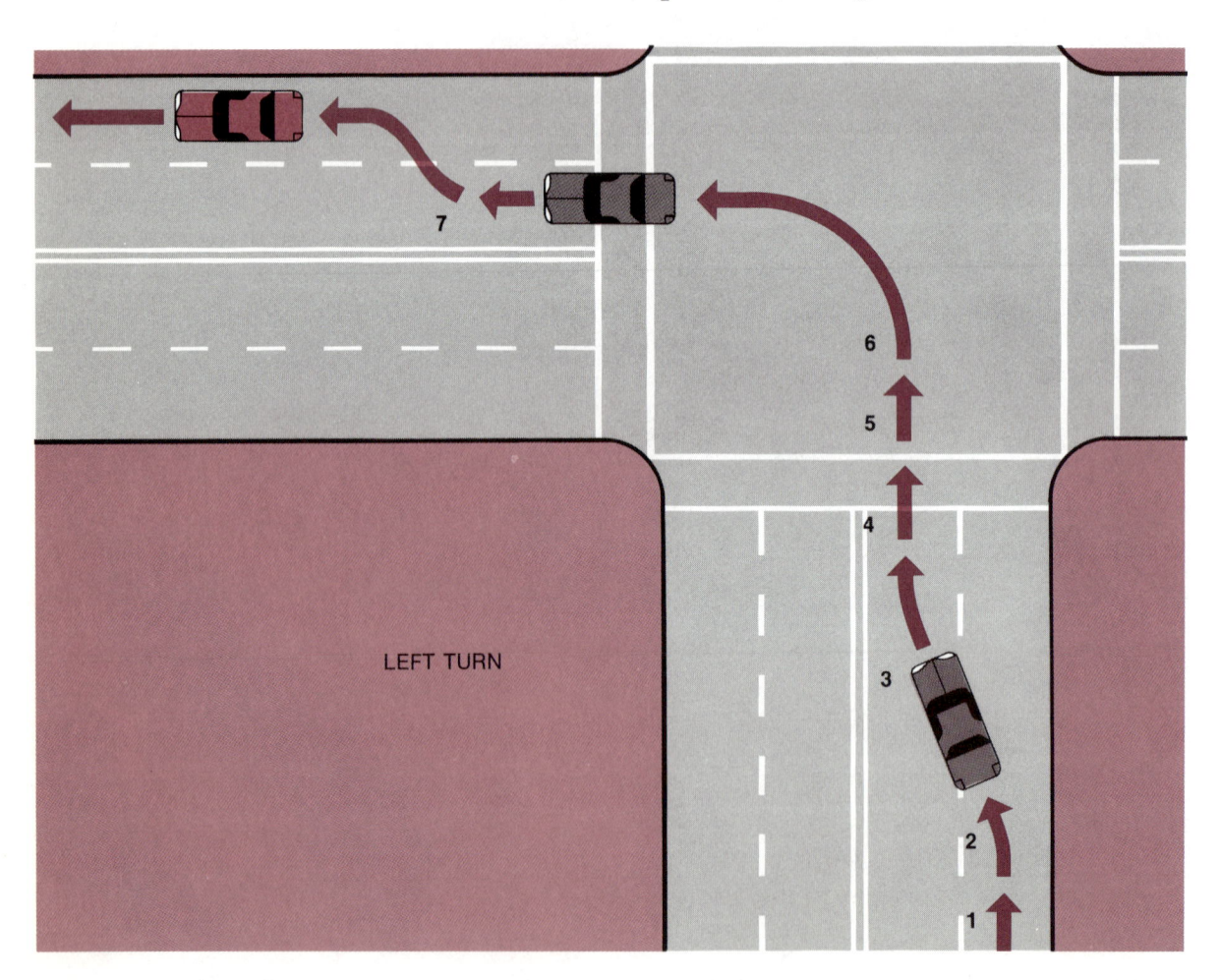

LEFT TURN

Backing

Before you back up, be sure there is nothing behind the car. The best way to be sure is to look before you get in the car. Watch out for children, pets, and bicycles.

Checking the rearview mirrors is not enough. When you are in the car, turn part way around. Look over your shoulder to see what is behind you. Steer with your left hand. The car will go in the direction you turn the wheel. If you turn the wheel to the right, the car will back to the right. If you turn it to the left, the car will back to the left.

This may seem easy enough to do. But backing takes a lot of skill. At first, you will have to keep thinking about which way to turn the wheel. Practice backing until you can steer "by the feel of it." Practice in a place where there are no pedestrians or other cars.

Backing with Automatic Transmission

After starting the engine, follow these steps:

1. Push down on the brake pedal.
2. Move the transmission selector to R.
3. Release the parking brake.
4. Check traffic in all directions.
5. Turn part way around. Place your left hand on the top of the steering wheel. *(These directions are for backing to the left. When backing to the right, steer with your right hand.)*
6. Take your foot off the brake. The car should begin to back. If it does not, press very gently on the accelerator. Back slowly and be ready to stop at any time.

Backing with Standard Transmission

1. Push the clutch pedal in all the way.
2. Shift to reverse.
3. Release the parking brake.
4. Check traffic in all directions.
5. Turn part way around. Place your left hand on the top of the steering wheel.
6. Press very gently on the accelerator. At the same time, slowly let out the clutch until it reaches the friction point.
7. Hold the clutch at the friction point for a second or two. Press down on the accelerator just a bit more. Let the clutch out the rest of the way.

Turning the Car Around

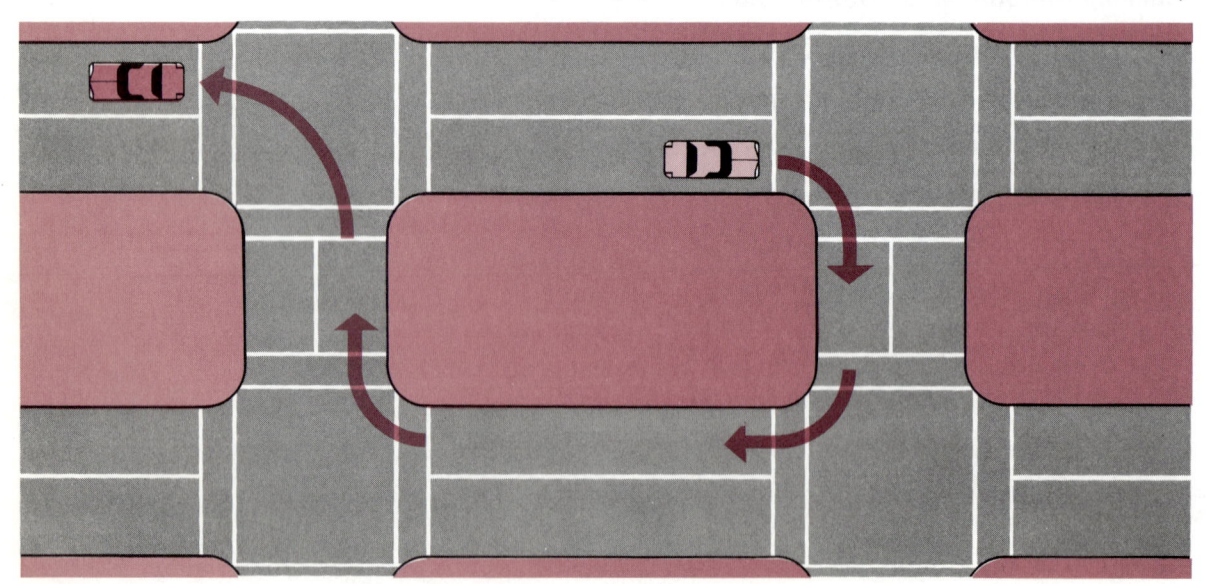

Sometimes the best way to turn around is to drive around the block. In city driving, this is often the only way you can turn around. But at other times, you may be able to make a U-turn or a three-point turn. Sometimes you can also turn around by using a side street. This is called an intersection turn.

The Alley or Driveway Turn

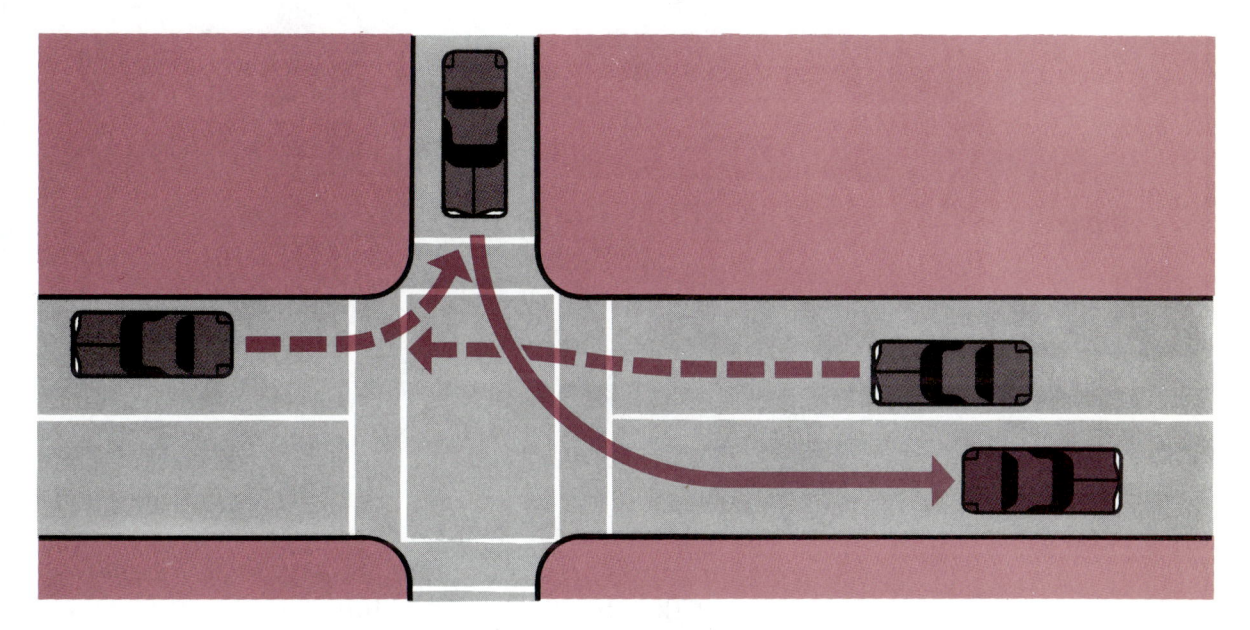

Always check traffic carefully before making this kind of turn. Be sure there are no cars or pedestrians behind you before backing up.

First drive past the alley or driveway. Stop. Then back into the alley. Stop with wheels straight.

Watch for pedestrians and other traffic. Signal for a left turn. Check traffic again. If it is safe, drive forward and turn left.

The U-Turn

If you are on a wide street, you can sometimes make a U-turn. But check traffic signs first. On many streets it is against the law to make a U-turn. Do not cross a double yellow line to make a U-turn. Do not make a U-turn close to an intersection.

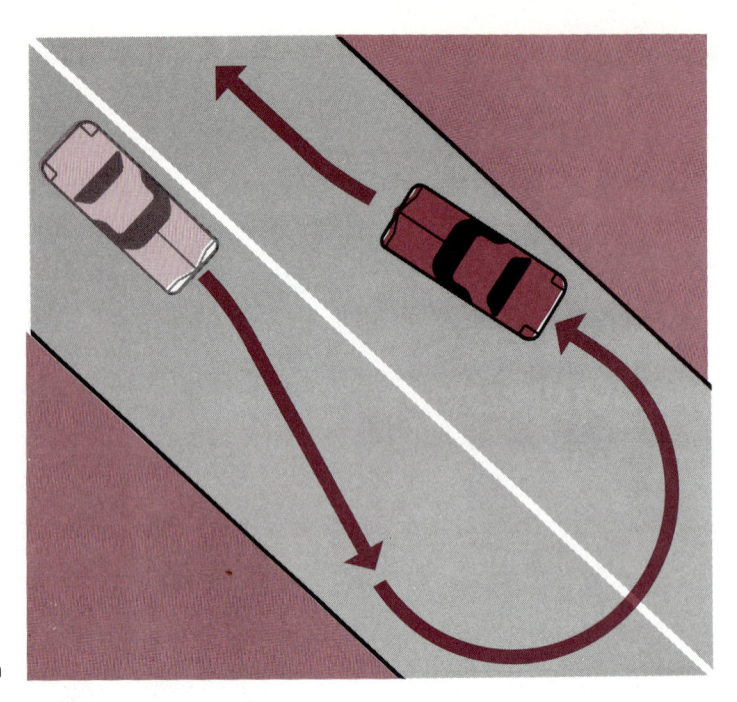

U-Turn

Check traffic first. Look out for pedestrians crossing the street. If it is safe, pull over to the right side of the street. Come to a full stop. Signal for a left turn. Check traffic again before starting.

As the car begins to move, begin turning the steering wheel to the left. Turn the wheel all the way to the left as quickly as you can. But do not begin turning the wheel until the car is moving. Turning the wheel when the car is stopped is bad for the tires. It is also hard on the steering system.

The Three-Point Turn

The three-point turn is also called the Y-turn. The three-point turn is used on streets that are not wide enough for a U-turn. Like the U-turn, the three-point turn should be made only if traffic is light.

After checking traffic, pull over to the right side of the street and stop. Check traffic in both direc-

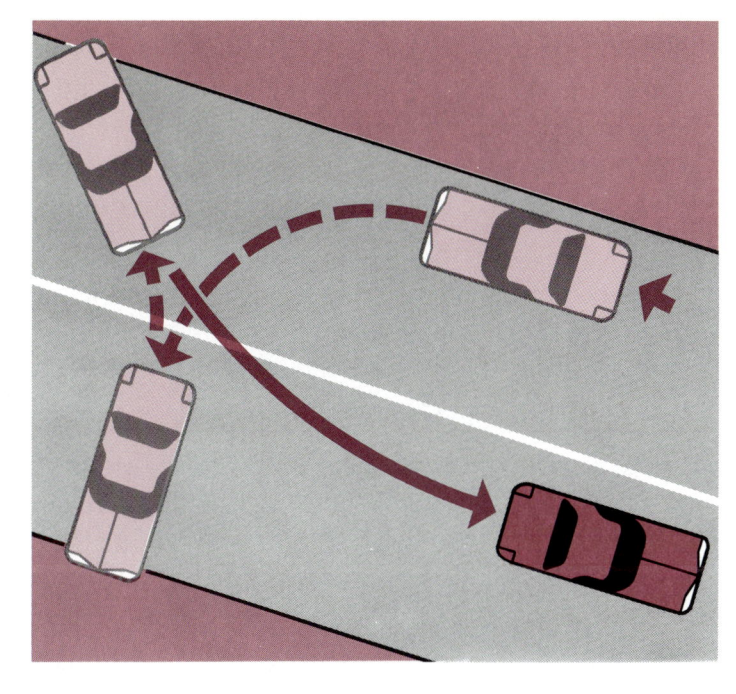

Three-Point Turn

tions. Signal for a left turn. If the way is clear, begin to move forward slowly. Start turning the steering wheel to the left as quickly as you can. When you are close to the curb on the other side of the street, stop. Check traffic again and then begin backing slowly. As the car begins to move, turn the wheel to your right as quickly as you can. Stop when the rear of your car is close to the curb. Check traffic. Then go forward and finish the turn.

Parking the Car

Learning to park is an important part of driving. To be a good driver, you must be able to park well. To be able to park well, you must have full control of your car. There are two kinds of parking—angle parking and parallel parking. Practice both until you are sure of your parking skills.

135

Angle Parking

Angle parking is used most often in parking lots. It is also sometimes used on wide streets where there are a lot of stores. Angle parking is not hard to do. But it still takes practice to do it right. Follow these steps:

1. Check traffic in both directions. Begin slowing down. The side of your car should be about 6 feet from the parked cars.
2. Signal for a right turn.
3. Keep an eye on the car parked to the right of your parking space. When the front of your car is even with the left tail light, turn right.
4. Drive slowly into the parking space. Brake gently until your right front tire just touches the curb. Do not run into the curb hard. You may damage your tire.
5. Shift to P or reverse and set the parking brake. Be sure to lock your car before leaving.

Check to see that the way is clear before pulling into a parking space. People often step out from parked cars without first looking to make sure it is safe.

Be careful when backing out of an angle parking space. On a busy street, this can be very dangerous. With cars parked on both sides, you will not be able to see much. Check the traffic as best you can. Then begin backing. Back up about 1 or 2 feet and stop. You will be able to see better from this position. If the way is clear, back up some more. Back up a little at a time. Keep the front wheels straight.

Back until the front of your car is even with the rear of the car on your left. Then turn the steering wheel to the right. When you are clear of the other parked cars, go forward.

Be careful when driving through a parking lot. The driver of a car backing out may not see you. Be ready to hit your brakes and sound your horn.

Parallel Parking

Most of the time you park on the street you will have to parallel park. Parallel parking is not as easy as angle parking. It takes more time to learn to do. But it is a skill you must know. After you have spotted a parking space, follow these steps:

1. Check the traffic. Signal that you are stopping.
2. Make sure the parking space is big enough. The space should be about 4 feet longer than your car.
3. Stop next to the car in front of the parking space. The back bumpers of the two cars should be even. The side of your car should be about 3 feet from the other car.
4. Shift to reverse. Begin backing slowly, turning the steering wheel to the right.
5. Keep backing until your car is at the angle shown in *Picture B.* Your steering wheel should be even with the rear bumper of the car ahead.
6. Continue backing very slowly, turning the steering wheel until the wheels are straight. Back until your front bumper is next to the rear bumper of the car ahead.
7. Turn the steering wheel sharply to the left. Back very slowly as you do this.
8. Stop and shift to D. Begin going forward slowly, turning the wheels until they are straight again. Leave some space between the car ahead and the car behind. Check to see that you are close to the curb. Your car should be about 1 foot away from it.
9. Shift to P and set the parking brake. Be sure to lock your car before leaving.

A Steps 1–3

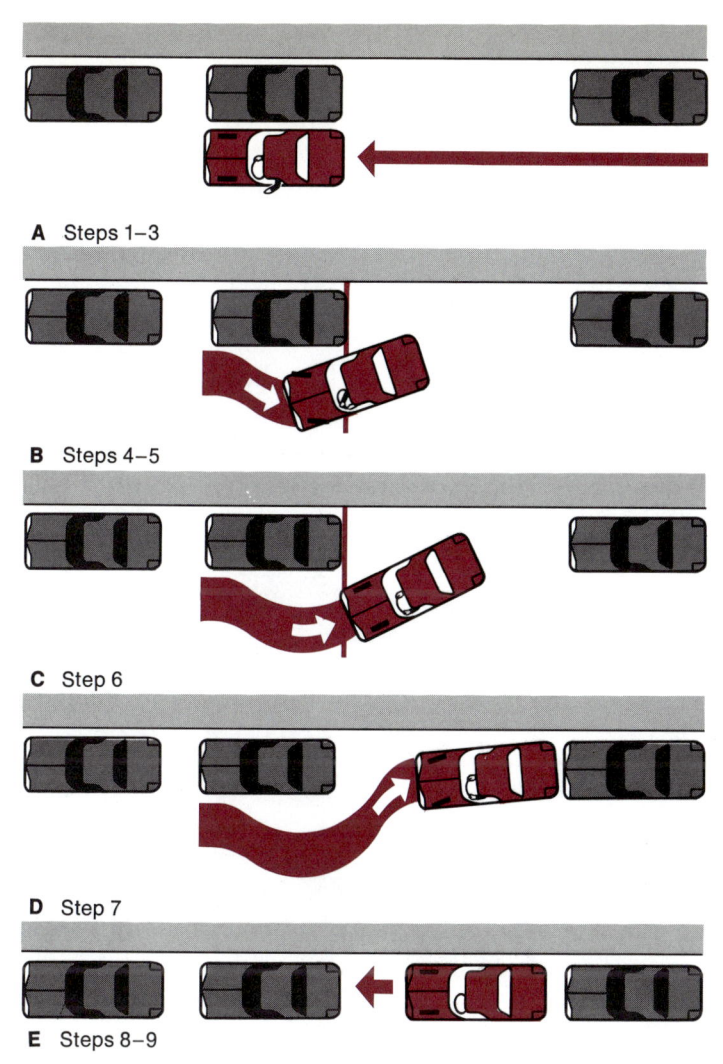

B Steps 4–5

C Step 6

D Step 7

E Steps 8–9

Getting out of a parallel parking space is not hard. First release the parking brake. Shift to R. Back slowly, turning the steering wheel sharply to the right. Shift to D. Check the traffic and make a left turn signal. Drive forward slowly, turning the steering wheel to the left. When you are sure you will not hit the car ahead, turn to the right. Keep turning until you are out of the parking space and going straight.

139

Parking on a Hill

When you park on a hill, make sure your car can not roll away. Be sure to park close to the curb. If you are facing downhill, turn the wheels sharply to the right. Move forward slowly until your right front tire touches the curb. Put the car in P and set the parking brake. With a standard transmission car, shift to reverse.

When parking uphill, follow the same steps. But turn your wheels *away* from the curb. Then let the car roll back until the front wheels touch the curb. Sometimes you may have to park on a hill where

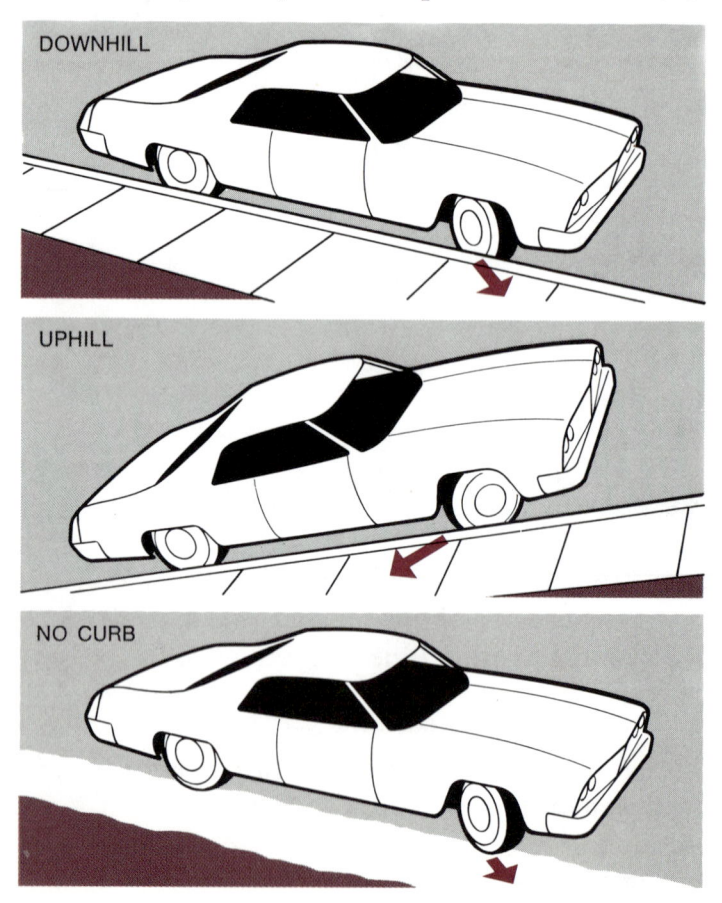

DOWNHILL

UPHILL

NO CURB

there is no curb. When there is no curb, always turn your wheels to the right. Do this for both uphill and downhill parking. Set your parking brake. Then put the car in P or reverse.

Starting on a Hill

Sometimes you will have to stop when going up a hill. If the hill is steep, you may have trouble starting up again. The car may begin rolling back down the hill. Or the engine may stop when you put the car in gear. Learning to start on a steep hill takes practice. If you are driving an automatic transmission car, follow these steps:

1. Keep your foot on the brake after the car has stopped. Set the parking brake. If you are stopping for only a short time, leave the car in D.
2. Move your foot from the brake to the accelerator. Press down on the accelerator until the engine begins to pull against the parking brake.
3. Check the traffic before starting. If you are going to turn, be sure to signal.
4. Release the parking brake and press down a little more on the accelerator.

If you are driving a standard transmission car, follow these steps:

1. Push in the clutch and keep your right foot on the brake. Set the parking brake.
2. With the clutch pedal all the way in, shift to first gear.
3. Push down on the accelerator. But do not race the engine.

4. Let out the clutch pedal until the clutch begins to take hold. Keep the clutch at this point. As the engine begins to pull, it will slow down. Give it a little more gas to keep it from stopping.

5. Check the traffic before starting. If you are going to turn, be sure to signal.

6. Push down a little more on the accelerator. Slowly let out the clutch pedal as you do this. At the same time, release the parking brake.

Starting on a hill with a standard transmission car is not easy. It takes a long time to learn. Pick a hill that is not too steep and practice starting over and over.

Checking What You Have Read

1. Suppose a driver is about to turn right at a corner. What can happen if he begins his turn too soon?

2. When making a right turn, about how far should your car be from the curb?

3. Suppose you are turning left at an intersection. What lane should your car be in after you have made the turn?

4. List all the steps you would follow in making a right turn.

5. Before backing up, what should you do to make sure the way is clear? Is checking the rearview mirrors enough?

6. Suppose you want to back to the right. Which way would you turn the steering wheel?

7. When should you *not* make a U-turn? Give three examples.

8. What is wrong with turning the steering wheel when the car is not moving?

9. When is it all right to make a three-point turn? When is it dangerous?
10. Why can backing out of an angle parking space be dangerous? What steps should you follow when backing out?
11. Suppose you are about to parallel park. About how far should the side of your car be from the parked cars?
12. Suppose you are parking facing uphill. Should you turn your front wheels toward or away from the curb? In which direction should they be turned when you are parked downhill?
13. Suppose you are parking on a hill with no curb. In which direction should you turn your front wheels?

To Talk About

1. When waiting to make a left turn, your front wheels should always be straight. What is the reason for this? What can happen if your front wheels are turned to the left?
2. The directions on p. 131 are for backing to the right. How would these directions be changed for backing to the *left*?
3. Some drivers open the door and look out as they back. Why is this a dangerous thing to do?

Things To Do

Find a street where there is parallel parking. Watch 10 or 12 different drivers park. Do some drivers have more skill than others? What kind of mistakes do you see? Do some drivers try to park in spaces that are too small? Bring a model car to class. Bring one that can be steered. Show the kinds of mistakes drivers make when parallel parking. Tell what drivers can do to keep from making these mistakes.

CHAPTER **10**

Driving in Traffic

Most of the driving you do will be in cities and towns. With other cars all around, you will have to think fast. Is that parked car going to pull out in front of you? Is the traffic light going to change from green to red? You will have to be quick in deciding what to do. Any mistake can mean an accident. You must have full control over your automobile.

When you began learning to drive, you had to think about each thing you did. *"I want to turn right . . . Is it time to put my turn signal on? . . . Am I close enough to the corner? . . . Should I begin turning now? . . ."* With practice, you built up your skills. You became more sure of what to do and when to do it. Now you are ready to use those skills driving in traffic.

Moving Along in Traffic

In the city there are cars everywhere. Traffic signs and signals help keep things moving. But each driver also plays a part in keeping things moving. City traffic moves best when drivers help each other.

As you drive, keep up with traffic. The driver who tries to go faster than the cars around him slows everyone down. All of us have seen this kind of driver. He is always changing lanes and trying to pass. Other drivers must brake to keep from running into him. He is a danger to himself and to others.

The driver who goes slower than the cars around him is also a danger. By holding up traffic he forces other drivers to pass him. He slows down traffic in his own lane. He slows down traffic in other lanes, too.

When traffic is heavy, cars often move much slower than the posted speed limit. But if everyone drives at about the same speed, traffic can still move smoothly.

No one much cares to drive in traffic as heavy as this. But most of these drivers have no other way to get to and from work. With more and more cars on the road every year, an answer to this problem must be found.

When traffic is not so heavy you can drive near the posted speed limit. But keep in mind that the speed limit is safe only under good driving conditions. Always drive at a speed that is safe for conditions. Slow down in bad weather. Slow down at night.

Safe Following Distance

Don't follow the car ahead too closely. Use the Two-Second Rule for following (see pp. 51-52). Always try to leave enough space between your car and the car ahead. In traffic, this is sometimes hard to do. Another driver may pull into the space ahead. When this happens, drop back. Don't tailgate.

Also watch out for the driver who tailgates you. Tailgating is very dangerous. But drivers who tailgate seem to learn this only after they have had an accident. Don't let a tailgater force you to go faster than you think is safe. Help him to pass if you can. If you can not, you may have to get out of his way. It is better to have to change lanes than to be in an accident.

Traffic Lanes

On many city streets painted lines mark the traffic lanes. Most of the time there are two lanes of traffic in each direction. The right lane in each direction is for slower traffic. The left lane is for faster traffic. Some streets have three lanes in each direction. On these streets, the lane closest to the center line may be for left turns only. Or the lane on the far right may be for right turns only.

Once you are in the lane you want to be in, stay there. Don't change from lane to lane. Change lanes only to pass or turn. If you want to turn, change lanes 200 to 300 feet before the intersection. In heavy traffic you may have to change lanes even before this.

When in the right lane, do not drive too close to parked cars. And always be ready to stop. A pedestrian may step out from between two parked cars. Or a person in a parked car may open a door in front of you.

One-Way Streets

Many cities have a system of one-way streets. On these streets all the lanes go in the same direction. One-way streets are marked with signs and arrows. When driving in the city watch for these signs. If you miss them, you may turn the wrong way on to a one-way street.

Traffic Signals

Traffic signals help traffic move safely and smoothly. As you know, a red light means stop. A yellow light means get ready to stop. And a green light means go (if it is safe to do so). Traffic signals tell you when it is your turn to go or stop. But just because a light is green does not mean the way is clear.

Always be careful when coming to an intersection. Even when you have the green light be ready to stop. Look both ways before crossing an intersection. Watch for cars making left turns from the other direction. Also watch for pedestrians. Pedestrians often cross against the light even though this is against the law.

Most traffic signals change every 30 to 60 seconds. Keep this in mind. Be ready to slow down and stop if the light changes from green to yellow. Don't try to "beat" a traffic light by speeding up. If the light turns red, you may not be able to stop in time.

On some city streets, the traffic lights are set for a posted speed. A driver going at this speed will "make" every light. Each light will change from red to green as he gets near it. Drivers going faster or slower than the posted speed do not make the lights. They must stop for one red light after another.

Traffic Police

In heavy city traffic, traffic police often help keep things moving at intersections. The traffic signals at the intersections may be working. But the police officer's signals are the ones you must follow. Make sure you know what these signals mean.

Intersections

Stopping

The good driver knows that intersections are dangerous. Most traffic accidents in the city happen at intersections. The good driver is always careful when coming to an intersection.

Suppose the traffic signal at the intersection is red. Begin to slow down while you are still some distance from the intersection. Take your foot off the accelerator and let the engine help brake the car. This saves wear on the brakes. It also warns the driver behind that you are going to stop. He can see that you are slowing down.

Check the rearview mirror. Is the car behind you following too closely? Has he seen the red light ahead? Signal that you are stopping. Gently begin to pump the brakes. Bring the car to a smooth stop.

Rear-end collisions happen most often at intersections. One car comes to a quick stop. The car behind does not stop in time. Sometimes the second car is following too closely. Sometimes the driver is just not watching what he is doing. He does not see that the car ahead is stopping until it is too late.

If there is another car stopped ahead of you, don't pull up too close behind him. Leave 4 or 5 feet of space or more. Then there will be less chance of bumping into him. Even a light bump may cause damage.

Stop just before you get to the crosswalk. Stopping in the crosswalk forces pedestrians to go around your car. They may have to step into traffic to get by. Stopping in the crosswalk can also put you in a dangerous spot. A bus or large truck making a left turn may run into you.

Starting

When the traffic light turns green, it is your turn to go. But make sure it is safe before you start. Check traffic in all directions. There may be a car coming from the left or right. Will he stop? Be sure before you pull into the intersection.

Also watch for pedestrians. Watch for people getting off buses. They may not know that the light has changed. If you are turning right or left, watch for pedestrians in the crosswalks. The pedestrians in these crosswalks have the right-of-way. There may be a WALK signal. Make sure the way is clear before you start your turn. If you don't, you may have to stop part way into your turn. The car behind could run into you.

Two-Way Stops

At many intersections, traffic is controlled by stop signs. Stop signs are not always as easy to spot as traffic signals. Parked cars may keep them from being seen until you are close to the intersection. Be ready. Watch for stop signs before each intersection.

Some intersections are two-way stops. One street is a through street. The other street is a side street. Drivers on the through street do not have to stop. They have the right-of-way. Drivers on the side street do not have the right-of-way. They must stop and wait until the way is clear.

When you see a stop sign ahead, begin to slow down. Make sure the driver behind knows that you are going to stop. Signal by tapping the brake pedal. Then gently come to a stop. Often there is a line painted on the street showing where to stop. Be sure you come to a *full* stop. "Almost" stopping is both dangerous and against the law.

Make sure the way is clear before starting again. Watch for pedestrians. Watch for cars on the through street in both directions. Judging the speed and distance of these cars is important. Give yourself more than enough time to cross the intersection. Don't force other drivers to slow down or stop to keep from hitting you.

Four-Way Stops

Drivers coming to a four-way stop from any direction must stop. As always, make sure it is safe before you start moving again. Watch for pedestrians. And watch for other cars coming to the intersection.

1. Yield the right-of-way to any car already in the intersection.
2. You may get to the intersection at the same time another driver does. When this happens, the driver on the left must yield to the driver on the right.
3. Yield to pedestrians crossing the intersection. Also yield to pedestrians about to cross.
4. If you are turning left, yield to the driver of the oncoming car.

Uncontrolled Intersections

Not all intersections are controlled. Many intersections do not have traffic signals or stop signs. Be very careful when coming to an uncontrolled intersection. Slow down and look both ways. Be ready to stop. Follow the right-of-way rules if there is other traffic.

Sometimes you will come upon a "blind" intersection. You will not be able to see if the way is clear. For example, a stopped bus may hide another car coming toward the intersection. Move into a blind intersection very slowly. Be ready to stop or yield. Don't go through a blind intersection until you are sure it is safe.

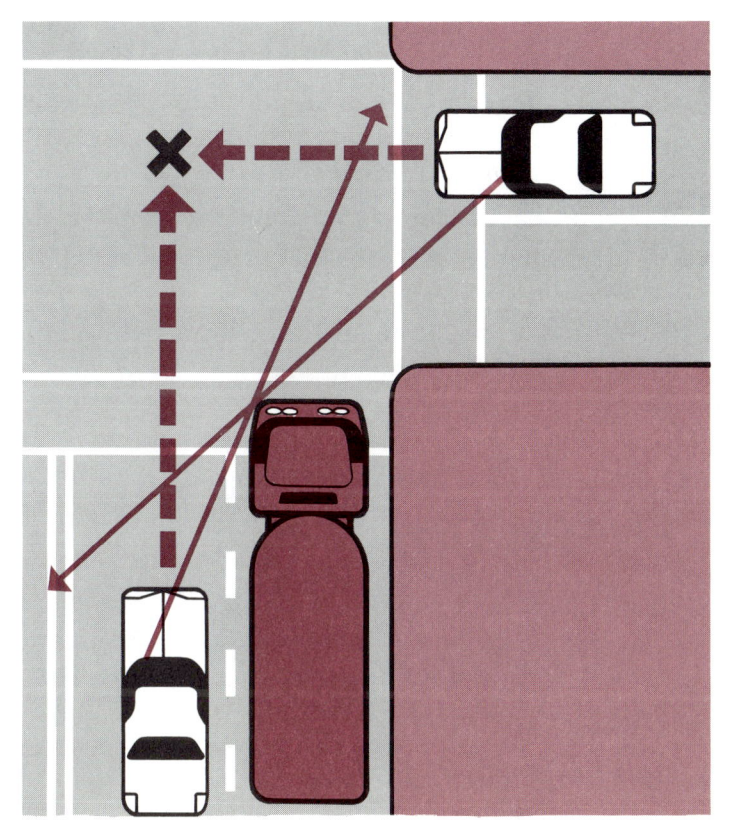

By blocking the view, the truck makes this a blind intersection for the drivers of both cars.

153

Checking What You Have Read _____

1. Why should a driver keep up with traffic? What happens when a driver does not keep up?
2. Is it always safe to drive at the posted speed limit? Give reasons for your answer.
3. What is tailgating? Why is tailgating dangerous?
4. Suppose you are driving along next to a line of parked cars. What kinds of things must you watch out for? Give two examples.
5. Why is speeding up to try to "beat" a traffic light a dangerous practice?
6. Why should you always signal to the car behind that you are planning to stop?
7. What is the reason for most rear-end collisions in the city?
8. At an intersection, you should stop before your car gets to the crosswalk. What is wrong with stopping *in* the crosswalk? Give two reasons.
9. Suppose you come to a four-way stop. When must you yield the right-of-way? Give four examples.
10. What is a blind intersection? Why are blind intersections dangerous?

To Talk About _____

1. Suppose you are driving in traffic. You are leaving a safe following distance. But then another car pulls into the space ahead. What should you do?
2. Everyone has seen drivers who keep changing lanes. This kind of driver is always trying to get ahead of traffic. He wants to "save time." Why would it be better for everyone if he stayed in his own lane? Does he save very much time by changing lanes?

3. On most streets there are lines painted to mark the lanes. But on many streets, there are no lines. Does this mean that there are no lanes? Does this mean drivers do not have to stay in lanes?

4. Most of the time it is best to keep up with traffic. But suppose most of the cars around you are going faster than the posted speed limit. What should you do then?

Things To Do ───────────────────────

Do a study of traffic conditions near your school. Which streets carry the most traffic? Which streets carry only a little traffic? Are most of the intersections controlled? Are there more stop lights or more stop signs? Which intersections seem to be the most dangerous? What can be done to make these intersections safer? What can be done to help traffic move more smoothly? Would one-way streets help? Draw up a plan to make driving near your school easier and safer. Tell about your plan in class. Does everyone in class agree with it? Be ready to give reasons for the changes you would like to see made.

CHAPTER **11**

The Pedestrian

When a car hits a pedestrian, the pedestrian is almost always hurt. One out of every 15 is killed. The pedestrian does not have much of a chance against an automobile.

We are all pedestrians part of the time. But not all pedestrians are drivers. As a driver, you must do all you can to keep from hitting pedestrians. As a pedestrian, you must learn to keep from being hit.

In Cities and Towns

Most pedestrians hit by cars are hit in the city. This is because there are more pedestrians—and more cars—in the city. Also, pedestrians are not always easy to spot in city traffic. The great number of cars, trucks, and buses often keep pedestrians from being seen.

Many pedestrians are hit at intersections. But even more are hit in the middle of the block. Drivers watch for pedestrians more closely at intersections. They are not as ready for them between intersections. It is dangerous to cross the street in the middle of the block. But many people do—and many are hit by cars.

When driving in a city or town, always be ready for pedestrians. Watch out for people crossing in the middle of the block. Most of the time these people do not have the right-of-way. But that does not mean they should be hurt or killed.

Watch out for children. A child will often run out into the street without thinking. When you see children around, slow down. If you see a ball roll into the street, get ready to stop. Most of the time a child will soon run after it.

Don't drive too close to cars parked along the street. A person in one of the cars might step out in front of you. Also look for people between parked cars. Children playing between parked cars are very hard to see.

Seeing and Being Seen

When you see a pedestrian, try to catch his eye. Make sure he sees *you*, too. Even on quiet streets, he might not hear your car coming. If you think he is going to step out in front of you, warn him. Give a light tap on your horn. But do not count too much on your horn. The pedestrian may be hard of hearing. Be ready to stop.

When you are a pedestrian, make sure the driver sees you. Keep in mind that a pedestrian is not always easy to spot in traffic. Don't step into the street until you know the driver has seen you. Even then, don't cross until you are sure it is safe.

Whom To Look For

The driver must watch out for *all* pedestrians. But some kinds of pedestrians are hit more often than others.

1. Old people are not as quick as other pedestrians. They can not see or hear as well. Also, many of them have never driven a car. Pedestrians who do not know how to drive get hurt more often

than any others. They do not know how much time it takes a car to stop. Because of this, they may think it is safe to cross when it is not.

2. Children do not know how dangerous automobiles can be. They run out into the street without thinking. They play between parked cars. They do not always look before crossing the street. As a driver, it is up to you to watch out for them. Slow down near schools and parks. Slow down when you see children playing.

3. The pedestrian who has been drinking alcohol (or taking drugs) is a danger to himself and to others. He can not think clearly. Often he does not know what he is doing. He may step in front of a moving car without looking. Again, it is up to you to watch out for this kind of pedestrian.

Busy intersections are dangerous both for drivers and pedestrians. When driving, watch for pedestrians before turning left or right. When walking, watch for cars before stepping off the curb.

The Most Dangerous Times

Most pedestrians are hit by cars between 4 and 8 P.M. This is the time of day when most people are leaving work. Both pedestrians and drivers are tired. They may not be as careful as they should be.

This is also the time of day when the sun goes down. It is harder to see things at dusk than at any other time of day. It is hard for drivers to see pedestrians. It is just as hard for pedestrians to see cars. Some drivers have their lights on. Others do not.

Night is also a dangerous time for pedestrians. A pedestrian can see the headlights of an oncoming car. But at night it is hard to judge how far away the car is. It is also hard to judge how fast the car is moving. Because the pedestrian can see the car, he may think the driver can see him. Often this is not

When you drive at night, watch closely for pedestrians. Slow down as you near intersections. When you are a pedestrian, try to make sure drivers see you. At night, wear light-colored clothes.

so. A driver might not see a pedestrian wearing dark-colored clothes.

When driving at night, do all that you can to spot pedestrians.

1. Keep your headlights and windshield clean.
2. Watch for pedestrians walking along the road in the dark. Don't look only where your headlights are shining.
3. Slow down at intersections. Look carefully for pedestrians before driving through an intersection. Also be careful when turning. Keep in mind that your headlights do not show you what is around the corner.

Watch out for pedestrians when driving on country roads. When you see a pedestrian, steer away from him if you can. Tap your horn to let him know you are coming. Slow down as you near him.

When you see a school bus ahead, be ready to stop. Be careful even when the bus is not picking up or letting off children. Don't follow the bus too closely. Keep in mind that school buses stop at all railroad crossings.

Bad Weather

In bad weather pedestrians often take chances they should not take. They may cross the street before the light changes. They may cross in the middle of the block. They may run to get out of the rain.

Rain or snow make it harder for the pedestrian to see oncoming cars. The driver has an even harder time spotting pedestrians. It also takes him longer to stop his car. And he might skid on the wet street.

You as a Pedestrian

As soon as you step out of your car you become a pedestrian. It is safer to get out on the curb side of the car. Getting out on the driver's side can be dangerous. Always look before you leave.

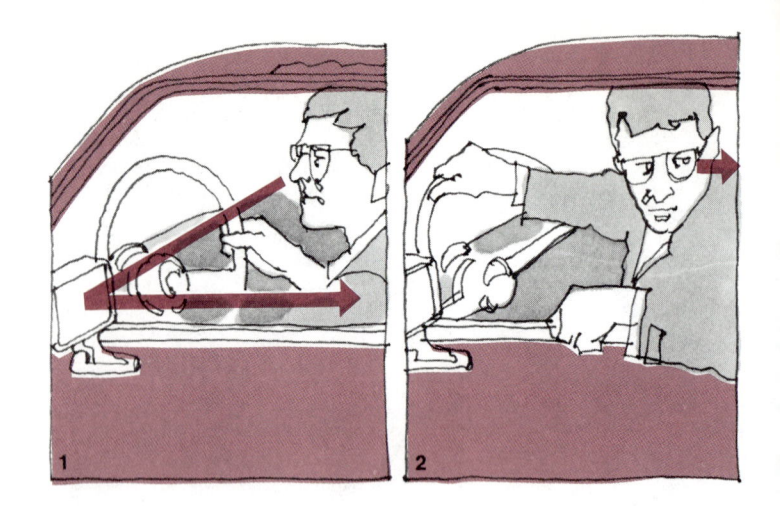

When getting out on the driver's side, follow these steps. First, check the outside mirror. Then look over your shoulder. If no cars are coming, open the door. Keep watching for cars as you do this. Step out facing traffic. Walk to the rear of the car, and then to the curb.

Rules for Safety

Just as there are rules for drivers, there are also rules for pedestrians. These rules should be followed by all pedestrians.

In the City

1. Check traffic in all directions before stepping off the curb. Even when you have the right-of-way, be sure to look before crossing.
2. Cross streets at intersections and crosswalks. Don't cross in the middle of the block.
3. Watch traffic signals carefully. Cross only when you have the green light or WALK signal. Don't cross if the light is about to change.
4. While crossing, look for cars turning right and left.
5. Never step out into the street from between parked cars.
6. Look around carefully after getting off a bus. Don't cross in front of the bus if there is no traffic signal. Wait until the bus pulls away before you cross.

Look both ways before crossing the street. Keep looking while you cross.

In the Country

1. If there are sidewalks or footpaths, use them. Don't walk on the road if you don't have to.
2. Always walk on the *left* side of the road, facing oncoming traffic.
3. Move away from the road when you see one car passing another.
4. At night, carry a light. Or wear something white. Do all you can to help make sure that drivers can see you.

Checking What You Have Read

1. Most pedestrians hit by cars are hit in the city. List two reasons why this is so.
2. Why is it dangerous to cross a street in the middle of the block?
3. If you blow your horn at a pedestrian, he will always know you are there. Is this true? Give a reason for your answer.
4. Old people are hit by cars more often than other pedestrians. Give three reasons why this is so.
5. Why should you be very careful when driving near schools or parks?
6. A person who has been drinking or taking drugs is not fit to drive. Is he fit to be a pedestrian? Give reasons for your answer.
7. What is the most dangerous time of day for pedestrians? Why?
8. At night, most pedestrians have little trouble spotting cars. Is it just as easy for drivers to spot pedestrians? Why or why not?
9. Suppose you are driving on a country road at night. Ahead, you spot a pedestrian walking along the road. For safety, what three things should you do?
10. Which side of the car is it safer to get out from? Give a reason for your answer.
11. Suppose you must get out on the driver's side. What is the safest way to do this? List the steps you would follow.
12. What can a pedestrian do to make himself seen at night? What kind of clothes should he wear?
13. In the country, on which side of the road should pedestrians walk? Give a reason for your answer.

To Talk About

1. If a driver breaks a traffic law, he can get a ticket for it. Do you think the police should give more tickets to pedestrians who break the rules?
2. It is often harder to see things at dusk than it is at night. Why is this? Why must a driver watch closely for pedestrians at dusk?
3. Sometimes pedestrians are hit by cars turning right at intersections. They are hit even though they are in the crosswalk and have the right-of-way. What can be done to cut down on this kind of accident? Are new rules at intersections needed?

Things To Do

Go to a busy intersection near your school. Watch pedestrians as they cross. Do most pedestrians follow the rules? How many cross against the light? How many cross in the middle of the block? Do most pedestrians look both ways before crossing? Also watch the drivers at the intersection. Do some drivers stop in the crosswalk? Do some try to "beat" the stop lights by speeding up? Write a short report about what you see.

CHAPTER 12

Highways and Freeways

There are many more cars in the city than in the country. And, as you might think, there are more accidents in the city. City driving can be dangerous. But driving on country highways is even more dangerous. Three times as many people are killed on country highways as on city streets. Why? Speed is part of the answer.

Safe Speed for Conditions

A person driving along on a highway may not think he or she is going very fast. 55 mph does not seem so fast on a smooth, straight road. But at that speed a car covers over 80 feet every second. Even under the best conditions, it would take the driver 247 feet to stop. Always drive at a speed that is safe for road, weather, or traffic conditions.

Keep in mind that the posted speed limit is for good conditions only. Slow down at night, or if there is rain, ice, or snow on the road. You may have to install chains. Be careful when coming to hills or curves or blind intersections. When you cannot see what is ahead, be ready for danger.

This does not mean that you should always drive slowly. A slower car holds up traffic and forces other drivers to pass. Go with the flow of traffic by keeping your car at the same speed.

Hydroplaning

If you go too fast in the rain with smooth tires, you may not be able to steer the car. Smooth tires act like a surfboard. They rise up on the water and lose contact with the pavement. If you feel this happening, keep the steering wheel straight and slow down. Avoid hydroplaning by keeping good tires on your car and watching your speed in the rain.

The drivers of these cars were not keeping a safe following distance. If they had been, this three-car rear-end collision might not have happened.

Safe Following Distance

Tailgating is dangerous on any road. But it is most dangerous on the open highway. Turn back to page 50 and you will see why. Faster speeds on the highway mean longer reaction distances and longer stopping distances.

Always keep a safe following distance between your car and the car ahead. Use the Two-Second Rule for following (see pp. 51-52). At slow speeds, one car length for every 10 mph should be safe. But at highway speeds even more distance is needed for safety. At 55 mph, leave seven *or more* car lengths following distance. In bad weather even this may not be enough.

Never tailgate. And try not to let another driver tailgate you. Keep checking your inside rearview mirror. If another driver is following too close, help him to pass.

Danger Ahead?

Hills

Be careful when driving up hills. Hills on two-lane roads are the most dangerous. You can not see what is on the other side of the hill. And drivers on the other side can not see you. A car might be coming over the hill toward you in your lane. The chance of a head-on collision is great. When nearing the top of the hill, keep well to the right of the center line. Be ready to pull off the road if you have to.

Let up on the accelerator when you get to the top of the hill. There may be a slow-moving farm vehicle ahead, or a stopped school bus. Watch your speed as you go down the hill. Use your brakes to slow the car. But do not keep your foot on the brake

Let up on the accelerator when coming to the top of a hill. There may be hidden danger ahead.

pedal. The brakes will get too hot if you do this. Slow the car by pumping the brakes. On steep hills you may have to shift down to second or low gear.

Curves

Check your speed as you near a curve. Often there will be a sign telling what the safe speed is. (In poor driving conditions this speed may still be too fast.) Also check the road surface. Is the curve banked, crowned, or flat? As you learned in Chapter 3, crowned and flat curves are the most dangerous.

Always slow to a safe speed before coming to a curve. Keep the car at this speed as you move through the curve. Then pick up speed again as you start coming out of the curve. But don't begin to go faster until you can see that the way is clear. Trees, or the side of a hill, may hide danger ahead.

Intersections

Intersections along highways are always marked. They are controlled by traffic signals or stop signs. But intersections are still very dangerous. A driver may cross the highway in front of a fast-moving car. Or he might not see the stop sign. Slow down before coming to an intersection. Look both ways before going through. You may have the right-of-way. But what if another driver does not see you coming? Don't take any chances. Be ready to stop.

Railroad Crossings

Most railroad crossings are well marked. The first warning is the round yellow and black RR sign. In the country, this sign is posted about 750 feet from the crossing. In the city, the sign is about 100 feet from the crossing.

Get ready to slow down or stop when you see this sign. Look around to see if a train is coming. Roll down your window and turn off the radio. Listen for the sound of a train coming. Often you can hear a train before you can see it.

Even when the way seems clear, slow down as you near the crossing. There may be light and bell signals at the crossing. There may also be a gate. There is always a black and white crossbuck. Often, a sign on the crossbuck tells how many tracks there are. Stop if the light signals begin flashing. Never try to cross when a train is coming.

Don't cross the tracks until you are sure it is safe. Look both ways and keep listening. If the way is still clear, cross the tracks. Cross at a speed of 10 mph or more. Go fast enough so you will cross all tracks even if your engine should stop.

Be careful if there are cars ahead of you crossing the tracks. Don't follow right behind the car ahead. If the driver stops, you may be caught on the tracks.

When you stop to let a train go by, be careful before starting again. Wait a few seconds after the train has passed. There may be another train coming on another track. Always make sure the way is clear before crossing.

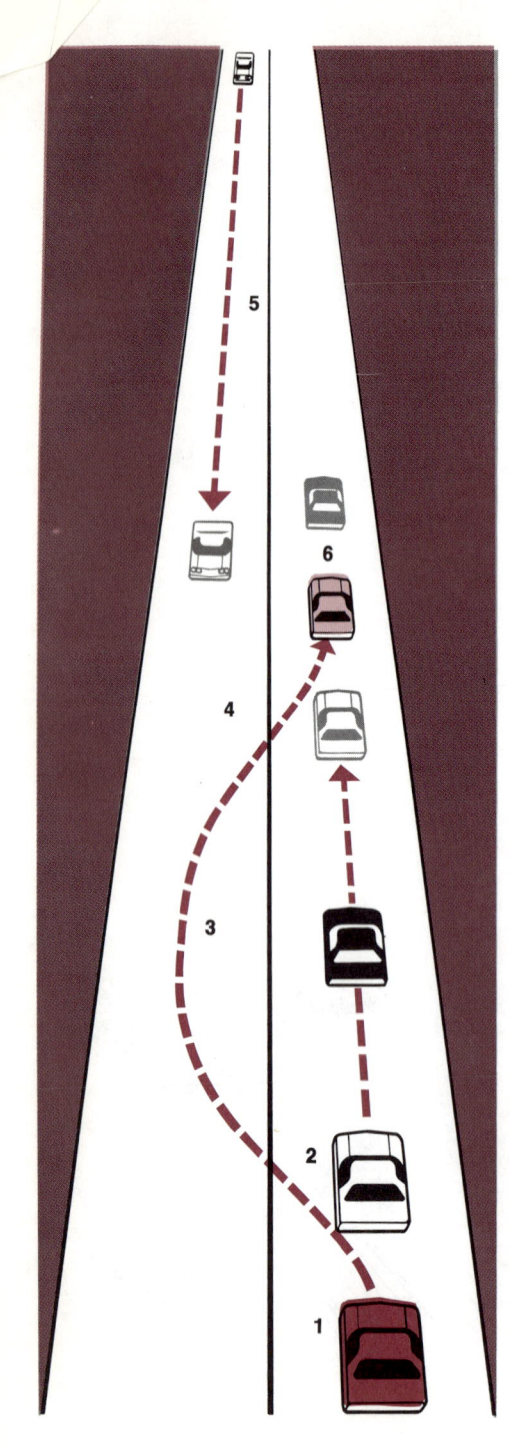

Passing

Judging Conditions

There is always some danger when one car passes another. Passing on any road can be dangerous. But passing on a two-lane road is the most dangerous of all. The chance of a head-on collision is always there. Before passing, you must judge:

1. your own speed
2. the speed of the car you want to pass
3. how long it will take you to pass and get back in your own lane
4. how much safe distance you have to pass
5. the speed of any oncoming car
6. the distance between the car you pass and the next car ahead

Judging the speed of an oncoming car is not easy to do. How fast is he coming toward you? Keep in mind that you are moving, too. Suppose you are driving at 50 mph. Suppose the oncoming car is also moving at 50 mph. Your car and the oncoming car are nearing each other at a speed of 100 mph. If you start to pass, can you get back in your own lane in time? Make sure you have enough time and distance. If you are not sure, don't pass.

No Passing Areas

It is against the law to pass in a no passing area. These areas are often marked with DO NOT PASS signs. Or they may be marked with lines painted on the road. A solid yellow line on your side of the road means no passing. A double yellow line also means no passing.

174

The pictures below show some no passing areas. Look at each picture. Can you see why passing is dangerous in each area?

How To Pass

Even if there are no signs or markings, it may not be safe to pass. Check all conditions before you start to pass. Look down the road ahead of you. Are you getting near a no passing area? Is there a bridge or an intersection ahead? Never pass if you think there is danger ahead. Wait until you are sure it is safe. When passing, follow these steps:

1. Check both rearview mirrors. Also check over your left shoulder. Make sure the left lane is clear before you pull out. Watch out for the car behind. He may be getting ready to pass *you*.

2. Put on your left turn signal. This will tell drivers behind that you are going to pull out. Be sure to signal *before* you start pulling into the left lane.

3. Begin passing from a safe following distance. Don't pull right up behind the car ahead before passing. If you get too close, you can not see as well. You are in danger of having a rear-end collision. And you have no room to get up to a safe passing speed.

4. Sound your horn as you begin to pass. At night, flash your lights. Make sure the driver of the car ahead knows you are passing him.

5. Pass at a speed of 10 to 15 mph faster than the car ahead. Pass quickly, but don't go over the posted speed limit.

6. Put on your right turn signal before pulling back into your lane. Be sure you don't cut off the driver you have just passed. Pull back into your lane only after you can see him in your inside mirror.

Before pulling out to pass, be sure you have enough time and distance to pass safely. If you are not sure, don't pass.

Freeway Driving

Today's highways are built for speed and safety. The fastest and safest of these new roads are the freeways. Drivers can drive at the legal speed limit for hour after hour without worry. They can travel 200 or more miles without stopping. Freeway driving is safe. There are only half as many accidents on freeways as on other kinds of highways.

Built for Safety

Freeways are built for safety. There is little chance for head-on collisions. The lanes going one way are divided from the lanes going the other way. Sometimes there is a fence between the two sets of lanes. Often there is a wide strip of land called a median strip. There are also fences on both sides of the freeway.

There are no intersections, side roads, or railroad crossings on freeways. There are no stop lights or stop signs. Cars can get on or off only at interchanges. Often there is a long distance between one interchange and the next.

For safety and better wear, check your tire pressure once a month or more. Never check the pressure when the tires are hot from running.

Before You Start

Freeway driving means fast driving. Be sure you are ready before you start. And be sure your car is ready. For high-speed driving everything must be in good working condition.

- *Check your tires.* Are they in good condition? Are the front and rear pressures right? Look for cuts on the sides of the tires. A tire in poor condition could blow out.
- *Check your brakes.* Does the car pull to one side or the other when you brake? Do you have to push the pedal to the floor to stop? Do you have trouble stopping? You should not drive on *any* road if your brakes are in poor condition. But on the freeway, good brakes are more important than ever.
- *Check your engine.* (Or have someone check it for you.) Is your fan belt in good condition? Worn fan belts often break at high speeds. Does the engine run smoothly? Are there any other problems?
- *Check your gas, oil, and water.* At high speed, your engine uses much more gas. And on many freeways gas stations are often miles from one another. If you are going a long way, fill up before you start. Put in more oil if you need it. And check the water in the battery and radiator.

When your car is ready, be sure you are ready, too. Look at a map before you begin. You can get one at almost any gas station. Plan ahead. At what interchange will you get on the freeway? At what interchange will you get off? You will not have much time to think about it once you are on the freeway. If you miss your exit, you may have to drive miles before the next exit.

Getting on the Freeway

First, be sure that the road you are on *is* an entrance road. Check the signs carefully. Sometimes drivers mistake an exit road for an entrance road. Nothing could be more dangerous. To keep this from happening, many exit roads are marked with red warning signs.

Also make sure that the entrance road is for the direction you want. If you want to go north, for example, make sure the entrance is marked NORTH. Entrance roads for both directions are often close together. It is easy to make a mistake.

Picking Up Speed

As the entrance road nears the freeway it becomes an acceleration lane. Speed up as you get to the acceleration lane. This is the time to bring your car up to freeway speed.

Put on your left turn signal. This helps drivers on the freeway see that you are coming. Be careful if there is a lot of traffic. Pick a space between cars where it is safe to enter. This calls for careful judging.

If traffic is very heavy it may be hard to find a space. Most of the time, other drivers will help you get into the line of traffic. They know that a car in

By the time a driver nears the end of the acceleration lane he should be up to freeway speed. A skilled driver enters the line of traffic smoothly, without forcing other drivers to brake.

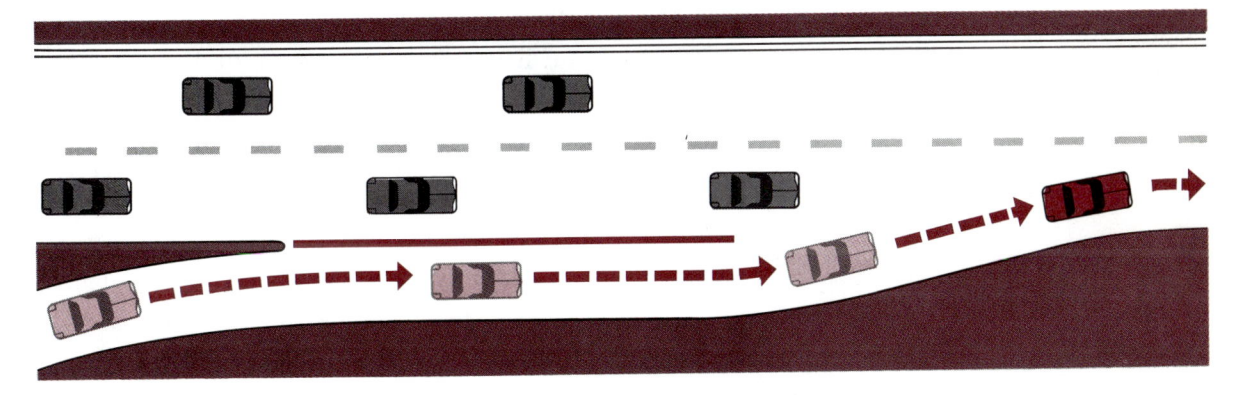

179

the acceleration lane *must* pull in. The driver has no place else to go. The acceleration lane soon ends.

Don't stop while in the acceleration lane. If you do, you will have to enter freeway traffic from a standing start. The chance of being hit from behind by a faster car would be great. You could also be hit by the car following you in the acceleration lane.

On the Freeway

Once you are on the freeway, keep up with traffic. Don't go faster than the posted speed limit. But don't go too slow. There is a minimum speed limit. It is against the law to go slower than this minimum speed limit. It is also dangerous. A driver going too slow holds up traffic. And he could be hit from behind by a faster car.

There are more rear-end collisions on the freeway than any other kind of accident. As many as 30 or 40 cars are sometimes damaged in these collisions. First, one car hits into the car ahead. Both cars stop. But other cars behind can not stop in time. Car after car run into each other. Most of the time, accidents like these happen when traffic is heavy. At such times drivers may not be keeping a safe following distance.

Don't follow the car ahead too closely. Use the Two-Second Rule for following. If another car pulls into the space ahead, drop back. Never tailgate. Also watch for cars tailgating you. If a car is following you too closely, slow down and let him pass.

Watching for Danger

As you drive keep an eye on traffic around you. Check both rearview mirrors every few seconds. There is a blind spot the mirrors do not cover.

Most of the drivers here are keeping a safe following distance. But a few are following too closely. If one of the drivers ahead must hit the brakes, there could be a rear-end collision.

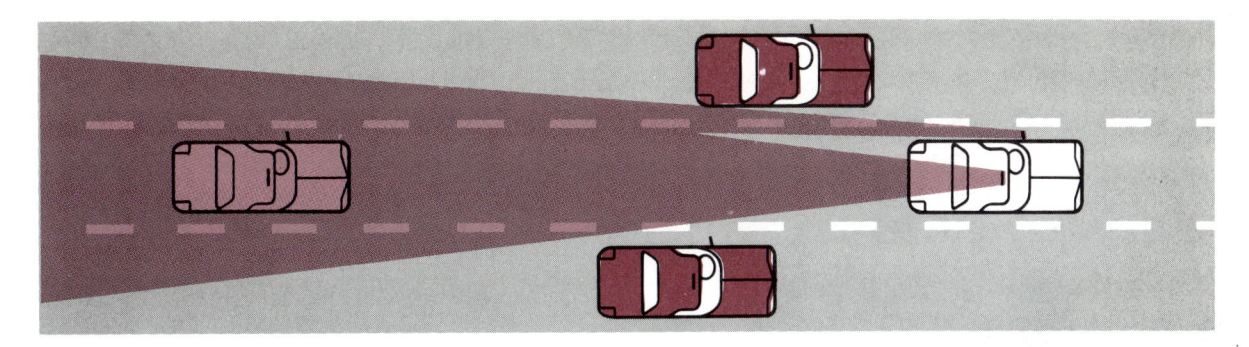

It is to the left and to the rear of your car. Look for a car in your blind spot before passing.

Try to see as much as you can. Don't just watch the car ahead of you. Watch the cars ahead of him, too. Be ready if you see someone's brake lights go on. If you think there is trouble-in-the-making, tap your brake lights. Let the driver behind you know that you may have to stop.

On the freeway a driver must watch for cars both on the left and the right. A car may be in the blind spot on his left. Another car, as here, can also be hidden on the right.

Passing

Freeways often have three or four lanes in each direction. The lane on the right is for the slowest traffic. The lane on the left is for the fastest traffic. Pick the lane you want to drive in and stay in it. As on any road, don't change lanes more than you have to.

Always be careful when changing lanes and passing. Make sure other drivers know what you are going to do. At freeway speeds, things happen fast. If you pull out without warning, you could have an accident. The driver in another car may not be able to react quickly enough.

Follow the same rules for passing that you have already learned. Look to see if the way is clear. Be sure to check your blind spot. Signal that you are changing lanes. Pass quickly, but don't go faster than the speed limit.

Breakdowns

Sometimes even a new car breaks down. A tire may blow out. Or something might go wrong with the engine. Learn what to do in an emergency.

1. Try to pull off on the right-hand shoulder, out of traffic. Get your car off the road if you can.
2. If your car has emergency flashers, put them on. At night, turn on the light inside your car. This will help other drivers to see that you are stopped.
3. If there is danger of your car being hit, put out warnings. At night, use flares.
4. Open your hood as a signal that you are having trouble.
5. Stay near your car, but stay off the road. Don't try to cross the freeway for help. Wait for help to come to you. Most of the time a police car will soon be along. The policeman can radio if more help is needed.
6. If you see another car stopped for an emergency, let the police know. Don't stop yourself. By stopping, you only make things more dangerous.

Leaving the Freeway

To drive safely on the freeway, you must plan ahead. You should know which exit you want before you start. If the road is new to you, check a map before starting.

Watch the road signs carefully. At high speed, you must learn to read them fast. As you near your exit, signal that you are changing lanes. Pull into the right lane when it is safe to do so. In heavy traffic, you may have to change lanes 1 or 2 miles before the exit. Signal again before you exit.

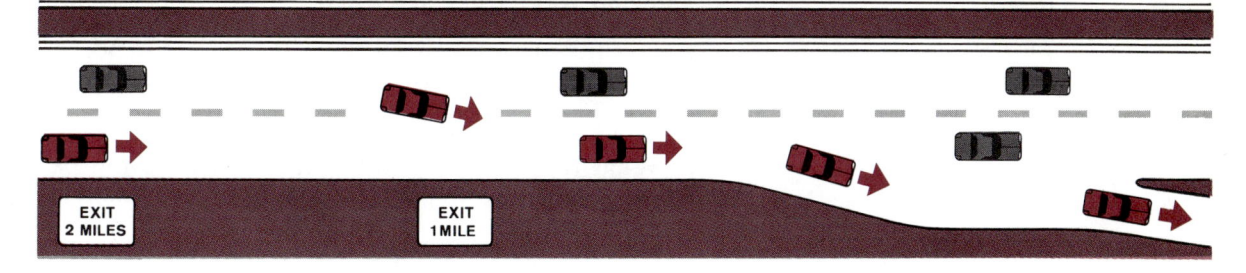

Keep up with traffic until you are on the deceleration lane. Once you are on the deceleration lane, begin slowing down. Watch the speed limit signs as you exit. Also watch your speedometer. After getting used to the high speed of the freeway, your exit speed may seem slow. But you may be going faster than you think.

Never stop and try to back up if you miss your exit. Backing on the freeway is a good way to get killed! If you miss your exit, drive to the next exit. You may have to drive a few more miles. But that is better than having an accident.

Move into the right lane a mile or more before the freeway exit you want. Be sure to signal before turning off into the deceleration lane.

Cloverleaf intersection

183

Checking What You Have Read

1. It is not always safe to drive at or near the posted speed limit. Give three examples when the posted speed limit may be too fast for conditions.
2. What rule should you use for following another car on the highway? How does this rule work?
3. When going down a hill, you should not keep your brakes on all the time. Why not? What should you do?
4. Suppose you are nearing a railroad crossing. What steps should you follow to make sure the way is clear? Name three or more things you should do.
5. Why is it always best to wait a few seconds after a train has passed?
6. List the six things you must judge before deciding to pass another car.
7. Why would it be dangerous to pass near a bridge?
8. What steps should you follow *before* you pull out to pass? List each thing you would do.
9. After passing, how can you tell when to pull back into your own lane?
10. Before driving on the freeway, you should check your car. What things should you check? Give five examples.
11. Why is it not safe to stop or slow down on the acceleration lane?
12. What kind of accident happens most often on freeways?
13. What is the blind spot?
14. What steps should you follow if you have a breakdown on the freeway?
15. What should you do if you miss your exit on the freeway? What should you *not* do?

To Talk About

1. Most cars can go 80 mph or 90 mph easily. Some can go much faster than this. Some people say there is no reason for cars to be able to go this fast. They think that cars should be made to go no faster than 70 mph. What do you think? Would limiting the top speed of cars help cut down on accidents?

2. Most drivers know that tailgating is dangerous. But rear-end collisions on freeways still happen all the time. Sometimes 30 or 40 cars may be damaged at a time. Can anything be done to cut down on this kind of freeway accident? Talk it over with others in class.

3. Why is it dangerous to drive in another driver's blind spot? Is there any way of knowing if you are in his blind spot?

Things To Do

Find out about the different kinds of freeway interchanges. Find out about the cloverleaf interchange, the diamond interchange, the trumpet interchange, and the partial cloverleaf. Draw large pictures of each kind. Tell about them in class. Use a model car to show how to get on and off each interchange.

CHAPTER **13**

Motorcycles

Each year there are more motorcycles on our roads. More and more people are riding motorcycles. They are fun to ride, and they do not cost much to own.

But motorcycles are also dangerous. They are much more dangerous to drive than automobiles. An accident with a motorcycle almost always injures the rider. Often he or she is killed.

The New Rider

A surprising number of those injured or killed on motorcycles are new riders. Many have accidents on their very first ride. All too often, they never have another chance to learn from their mistakes.

A passenger on a motorcycle should also wear a helmet. Riding without a helmet is dangerous—and against the law in many places.

Before a person rides a motorcycle in traffic, he should know the danger he faces. He should know what his motorcycle can do—and what it can not do. And he should keep in mind that riding skill takes a long time to learn.

The new rider often thinks he has more skill than he does. He learns to start, shift, and stop his motorcycle. He learns to turn corners. And often he thinks this is all there is to it. Everything he does seems just right—to him. In no time at all he sees himself as a great rider. He may even begin believing he is the best rider the world has ever seen! And he will keep right on believing it until he is killed or injured.

It takes time to build riding skill. The good rider knows this. He knows that his motorcycle is not a toy. Playing with speed and power can be a game that kills. He has fun riding, but he always rides with care. He knows that one mistake is all it takes. One mistake could kill him.

Protection for the Rider

An automobile is big, heavy, and strong. In an accident, it helps to protect the driver and passengers. Though the car may be damaged, the people inside are not always hurt. A motorcycle gives no such protection. In an accident, the rider is thrown off. He is almost always hurt. If he lands on his head, as often happens, he may be killed.

The rider must do what he can to protect himself. The good rider wears a helmet at all times. (In many states the law says a rider *must* wear a helmet.) Goggles protect his eyes, and gloves protect his hands. The clothes he wears help protect his skin from cuts if he falls. And heavy shoes or boots protect his feet.

But even this protection is not much in an accident. So the good rider does all he can to keep out of trouble. He keeps his motorcycle in good working condition. He checks his tires, brakes, and lights before riding. He makes sure his rearview mirror is in the right position. He does his best to see—and be seen.

Helmet, face protection, boots, gloves, and heavy clothes—if you are planning to ride a motorcycle, give yourself as much protection as you can.

Staying in Control

A car has four wheels—a motorcycle has only two. Because of this, skids are very dangerous on a motorcycle. A car can skid without always having an accident. The driver has time to get back in control. It is not the same with a motorcycle. The rider has little chance of bringing his motorcycle back under control. He is down before he can do anything about the skid.

The good rider always watches the condition of the road. He does not have as much control over his motorcycle as a driver does. A motorcycle skids much more easily than a car. Sand or gravel on the road mean danger. Water and oil are just as dangerous.

Because of the danger of skidding, many riders will not ride in bad weather. If they must, they keep their speed down and try to stay out of traffic.

Seeing and Being Seen

There are more motorcycles than ever on our roads. But many drivers still have not learned to look out for them. Some drivers think that roads are made only for cars. They feel that the motorcycle has no place on the road. Such thinking makes riding a motorcycle in traffic all the more dangerous. Most drivers would not make a left turn in front of an oncoming truck. But many will turn in front of an oncoming motorcycle. Because motorcycles are small, many drivers just *do not see them.*

The good rider knows this. In traffic he watches the drivers around him closely. Suppose he spots an oncoming car with its left turn signal on. Does

Many car-motorcycle collisions are caused by drivers turning left in front of oncoming motorcycles. Often, the driver does not even see the motorcycle until it is too late.

the driver see the motorcycle? What if he does not? The rider slows down. He gets ready to stop if the car should turn.

As a driver, you should learn to watch for motorcycles. A driver may hit a motorcycle because he does not see it. But often, he does not see it because he is *not looking for it*. Watch for motorcycles before you turn or change lanes. Keep in mind that there may be a motorcycle hidden in your blind spot.

Following and Passing

When driving behind a motorcycle, keep a safe following distance. A motorcycle can stop more quickly than a car. It also skids more easily. If you are following too closely and the rider should fall, you could run him over.

A motorcycle is not wide like a car. But this does not mean you can use part of the rider's lane when passing. Pass a motorcycle as you would pass a car. Leave enough room. Don't force the rider to pull over to the right as you pass.

Drivers must also watch out for motorcycles when passing other cars. The space in front of a car a driver wants to pass may seem clear. But there may be a motorcycle in the space ahead. Because it is small, the driver may not see the motorcycle until it is too late.

Safe Riding

If you plan to ride a motorcycle, learn the rules for safe riding. Many of the rules are the same for driving a car. But others are for motorcycles only. In some states, a rider must keep his headlight on at all times. This makes it easier for drivers to see him.

In many places, it is against the law to ride without a helmet. Check the laws before learning to ride.

Be careful when coming to a railroad crossing. If your front wheel gets caught on the track, you could lose control. Always cross railroad tracks at a right angle.

Stay near the left side of the lane you are in. Drivers might not see you if you ride along the right side of the road. Never ride between lanes of moving traffic. Some riders do this to get ahead of slow-moving traffic. It is a dangerous thing to do. Riding between lanes of traffic is also against the law.

Don't ride right next to another motorcycle. Stay a few feet in front of or behind the other rider. This gives both riders room if there should be an emergency. Always leave yourself room to get out of trouble.

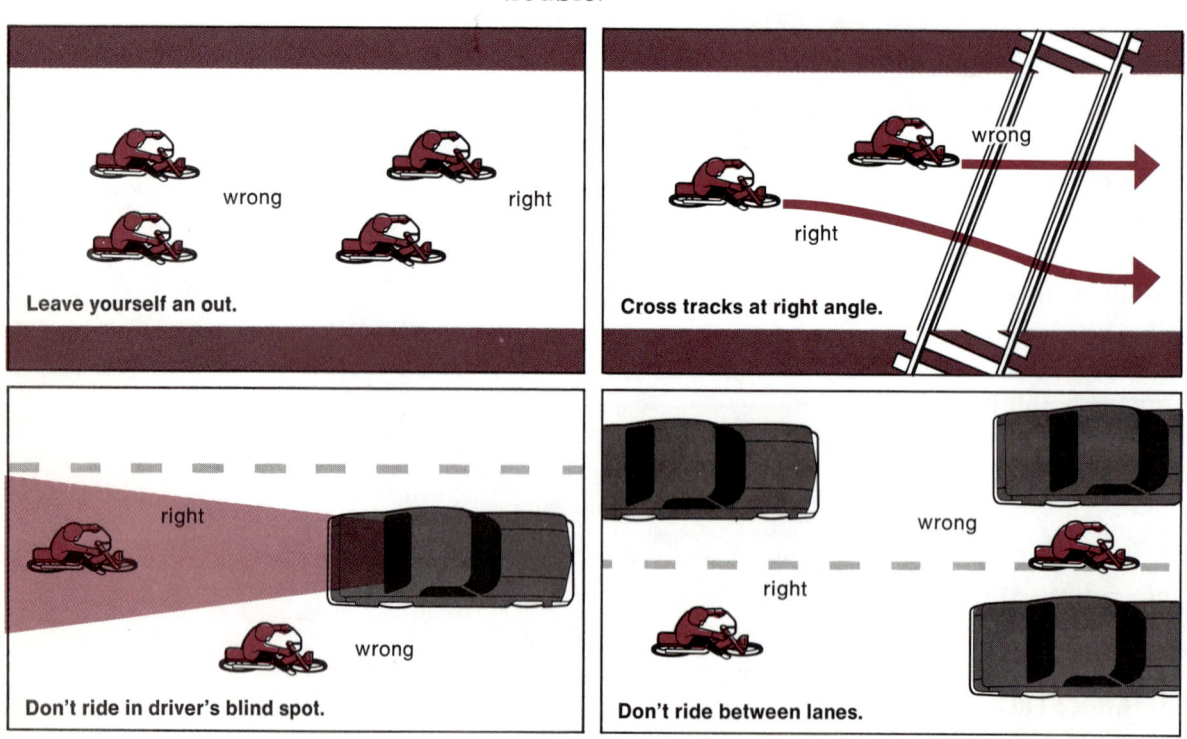

Leave yourself an out.

Cross tracks at right angle.

Don't ride in driver's blind spot.

Don't ride between lanes.

Checking What You Have Read

1. Many of those persons hurt or killed on motorcycles are new riders. Why do new riders have so many accidents?
2. Which gives more protection in an accident, an automobile or a motorcycle? Why?
3. What can a rider do to protect himself from being hurt on a motorcycle? What should he wear?
4. Why is skidding on a motorcycle so dangerous?
5. In traffic, a motorcycle rider should stay in the left part of his lane. Why?
6. At what angle should a motorcycle cross railroad tracks? Give a reason for your answer.
7. Why is it dangerous for a person to ride his motorcycle between lanes of slower moving traffic?

To Talk About

It is not hard to learn to operate a motorcycle. But it takes much more time to build up riding skill. Many new riders think they have more skill than they do. This is one reason why so many new riders are killed or injured each year. What can be done about this problem? Would motorcycle safety education help? Are new licensing laws needed? Talk it over with others in class.

Things To Do

Talk to someone who has owned a motorcycle for a long time. What has he learned about riding since he first started? Has he ever been in an accident or taken a fall? What was the reason for the accident or fall? What does this person do to protect himself when riding? What kind of helmet does he think is best? What kinds of mistakes does he think new riders make most often? Write a short report about what you learn.

CHAPTER **14**

Ready for Anything

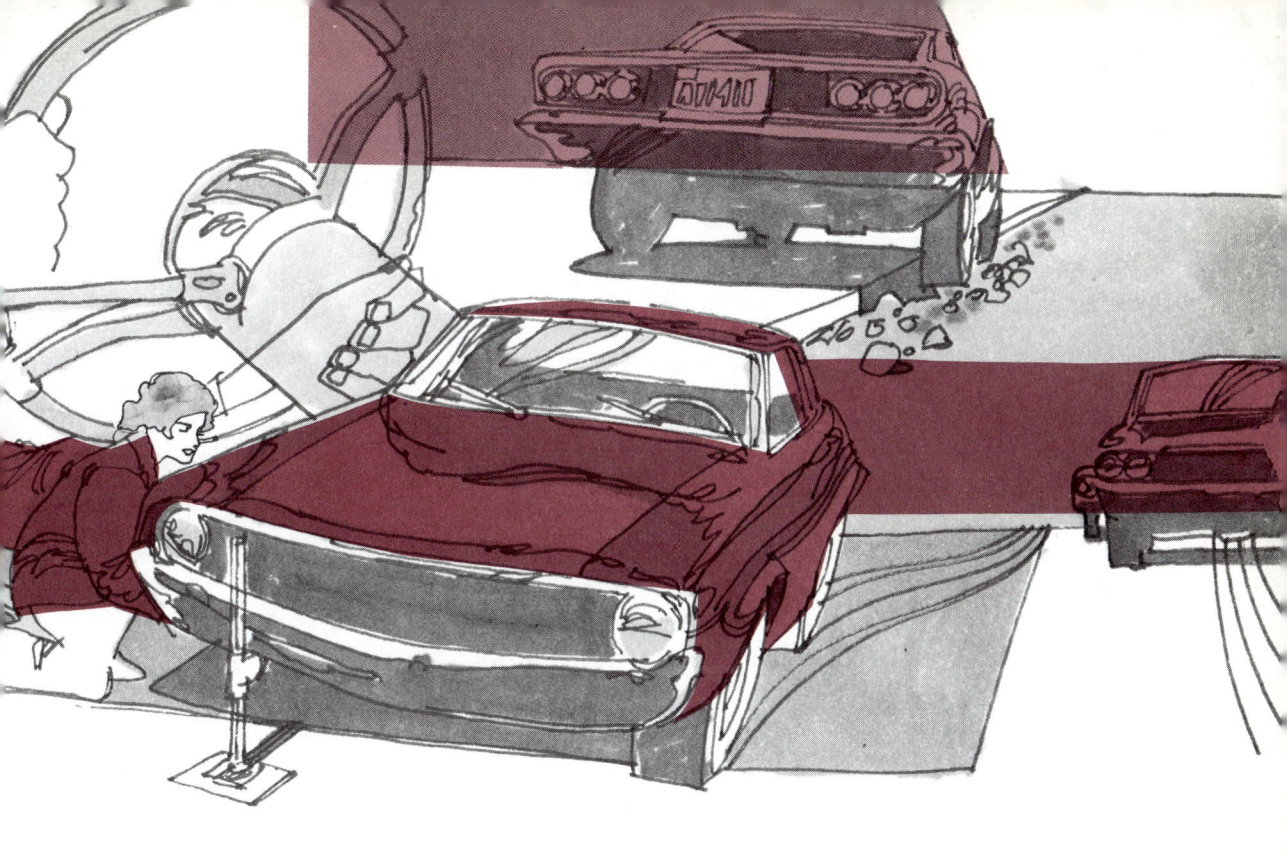

Most accidents happen because a driver makes a mistake. But even if you never made a mistake, you could still be in an accident. Another driver might make the mistake. For safe driving, you must become a defensive driver. You must be ready for anything.

The IPDE Process

A good way to be ready for anything is to learn the IPDE process. IPDE stands for *Identify, Predict, Decide, Execute.*

The first step in the process is to *identify* problems or possible problems. For example, as you are driving, you see an oncoming car just ahead. The car is slowing down. Why? You identify the car as a possible problem.

Next, you *predict* what the driver of the oncoming car might do. You predict that the driver has slowed down to make a left turn in front of you.

The next step is to *decide* what to do. If the driver of the other car turns in front of you, you may have to brake.

Finally, you *execute*, or carry out, what you have decided to do. The other driver turns in front of you. You brake so that you will not hit the other car.

As another example, let's say you see a traffic signal ahead. The light is green. But you *identify* it as a possible problem. Will it still be green by the time you reach the intersection?

Next, you *predict* what might happen. After watching the light for several seconds, you predict it will turn yellow before you reach the intersection.

Then you *decide* what to do. You decide to take your foot off the accelerator pedal and cover the brake pedal. Then you will be ready to stop if the light changes.

Finally, you *execute* what you have decided to do. You are ready to stop if the light changes.

Look at the pictures on page 197. Use the IPDE process to tell what you would do. First, identify the problem or possible problem. Next, predict what might happen. Then decide what you would do. Finally, execute, or carry out, what you would do about the problem.

Defensive Driving

The IPDE process will help you become a defensive driver. It will help you to protect yourself,

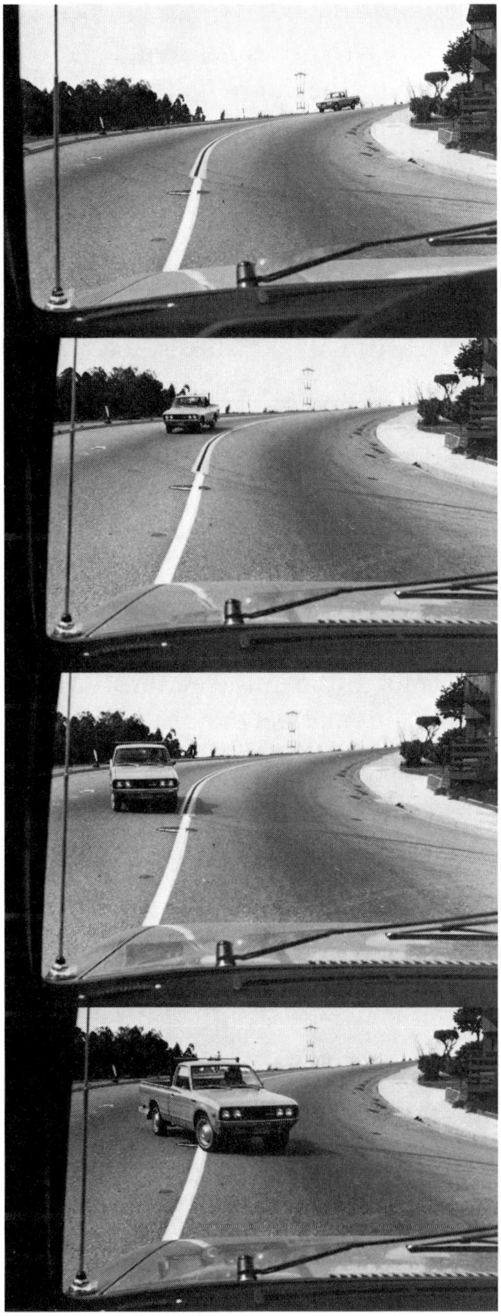

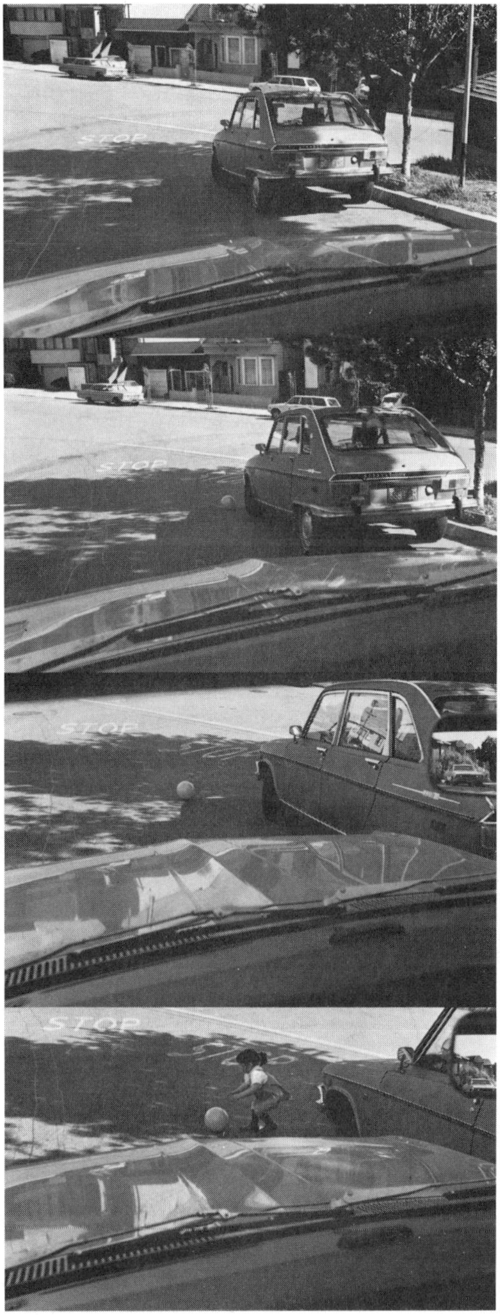
STOP

your passengers, pedestrians—*and other drivers.* That is what defensive driving is all about.

The more you drive, the more you will learn about defensive driving. If you are a good driver, you will keep on learning year after year. You will learn more about other drivers. And you will learn more about yourself. You can start now.

Know yourself. Know how much skill you really have—not just how much you *think* you have. Understand that you will make mistakes, too. Try to learn from your mistakes. That way, you will not make the same mistakes again and again.

When you drive, keep your mind on your driving. Think about what you are doing. Some drivers change lanes or make turns without looking. These drivers are not thinking.

Think ahead. Look for trouble-in-the-making. There may be hidden danger even when the way seems clear. Watch for blind intersections. Watch for pedestrians and animals on the road at night. When you cannot see very far ahead, always be

Collision ahead! Defensive driving could have kept this from happening. The driver of the car turning left should have checked his outside mirror before turning. The other driver should not have tried to pass two cars at a time.

ready for danger. If there should be danger, be sure that you can stop in time. Watch your speed. Always drive at a speed safe for conditions.

Watch out for the other driver. All drivers make mistakes now and then. Be ready for their mistakes. Watch for cars at intersections. You may have the right-of-way. But another driver might not see the traffic signal. Having the right-of-way does not always mean the way is clear. If there is danger ahead, yield the right-of-way.

Sometimes a driver may have a turn signal on and not know it. You cannot be sure if the driver knows the turn signal is on or not. You may think the driver is going to turn. But what if he or she does not turn? Don't cross in front of the other driver until you know it is safe to do so.

Leave yourself an out. Keep enough room between your car and the other cars on the road. Follow the car ahead at a safe distance. And watch out for tailgaters behind you. When you see a lot of cars ahead all driving together, drop back. Don't let yourself get boxed in by other cars. If one of the drivers has trouble, you may have no way to get around his or her car. Always leave yourself an out.

Make sure others see you. Watch other drivers and pedestrians closely. A driver who does not see you may turn into you. A pedestrian who is not watching may step in front of you. Let others know that you are coming. When you are not sure someone sees you, tap your horn. At night, you can also flash your lights. But even then, be ready to yield or stop.

Give yourself more than enough time. On any trip, leave a little early. If any problems come up, you will have enough time to work them out. You will not feel as though you have to hurry.

Ready For Anything

As a defensive driver, you must keep in mind that road conditions change. Sometimes you may have to drive when conditions are very poor. You will need all your skill to drive safely. You will need to be ready for anything.

Night Driving

Things are a lot harder to see at night. Your headlights show you only a little of what is ahead. And they can not show you what is around a corner or a curve. Always slow down when driving at night. Many accidents happen because drivers overdrive their headlights.

Overdriving headlights means driving too fast to stop in the distance you can see. Let's say your headlights are aimed right and are in good condition. They will light up the road up to 350 feet ahead of your car. At 50 mph on a dry road, you need about 243 feet to stop. But at 60 mph you need almost 370 feet. At 60 mph you would be overdriving your headlights. If there was danger ahead, you would not be able to stop in time.

A person who overdrives his headlights has no way of knowing what danger may be ahead.

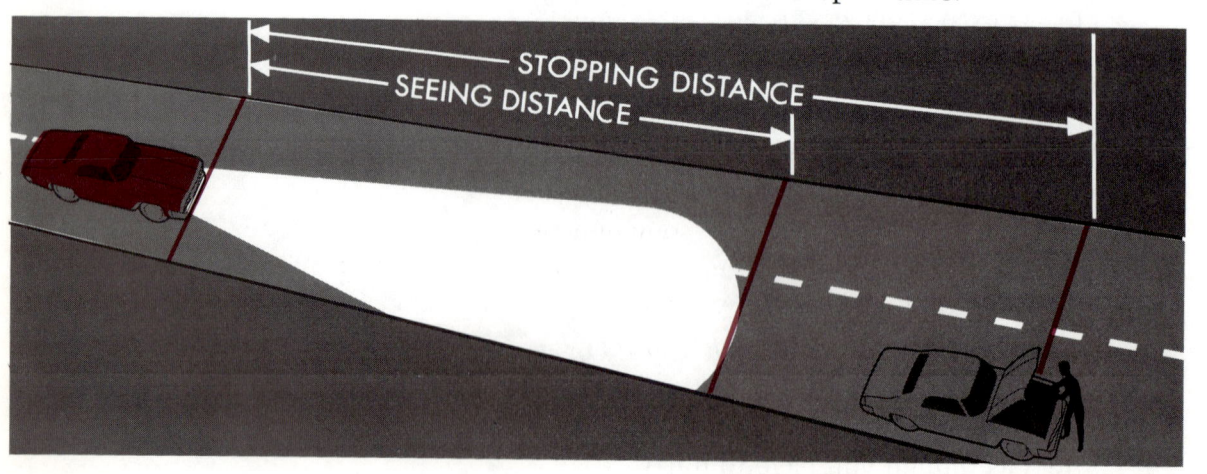

Your high beams will give you a better view of what is ahead. Use them if there is not much traffic around. But be sure to dim them when you see an oncoming car. The high beams can blind the other driver. Also dim your lights when following another car.

The driver of an oncoming car should always dim his lights. But if he does not, do not look straight at them. Look ahead and to the right until the car goes by. Watch the lane markings or the side of the road to help you steer. Look up again only after the other car has gone by.

Look for pedestrians walking along the road or crossing it. A pedestrian wearing dark clothes is hard to see. In the country, also watch for deer and other animals.

Before driving at night, make sure your car is in good working condition. Check your headlights. It is against the law to drive with only one headlight. Be sure both are working and aimed right. And be sure they are clean. Also check your tail lights and brake lights.

It takes only a few minutes to have your headlights aimed. Most service stations can do it for you while you wait.

Bad Weather

Driving in bad weather is not much fun. It is quite dangerous. Things are much harder to see. There is danger of skidding. And you need much more stopping distance. But sometimes you may have to drive in bad weather. Build up your driving skills so you will be ready. Keep your car ready, too.

Make sure your windshield wipers are in good condition. If they do not clean the windshield very well, have new ones put on. Also check your heater and defroster. The defroster should keep the windshield clear. Opening a window a little will also keep the windshield from fogging up.

Turn on your headlights in heavy rain or fog. But do not use your high beams. Fog will only throw the light back at you. Your low beams will help you to see a little better. And they will help other drivers and pedestrians see *you*. In very heavy fog, you may be able to see only a few feet. At such times, it is best to pull off the road and stop. Wait until you can see better before starting again.

Snow

When driving on snow-covered roads, use snow tires or chains. They make it easier for you to stop. They also keep you from skidding so easily. Keep a bag of sand in the back of your car. It is a big help if you get stuck in the snow.

If you get stuck, don't spin your wheels. Spinning your wheels will only make it harder for you to get out. Put some sand under the rear wheels. Make sure the front wheels are straight. Put the car in low. Then press *gently* on the accelerator. Keep changing from low to reverse until the car is out of the snow. This is called "rocking" the car out.

When rocking a car out of snow, try to keep your wheels from spinning. If the wheels begin to spin, reverse direction.

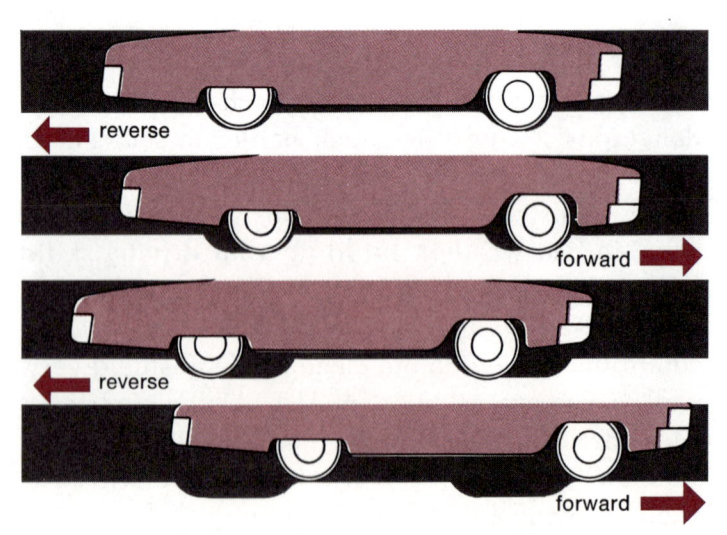

Emergencies

At some time or other, every driver is faced with an emergency. As a defensive driver, you will be ready. You will know what to do. You will know how to keep things under some control.

Skidding

There is always some danger of skidding. A car can skid even on a dry road. Coming around a curve too fast can cause a car to skid. Worn tires are also responsible for many skids. But most skids happen on wet roads. Water on the surface of the road can cause a car to skid. Snow- or ice-covered roads are even more dangerous.

Always slow down when there is danger of skidding. Slowing down is the best way to keep out of trouble in bad weather. But if you do skid, you should know what to do about it.

Turn the steering wheel in the direction the rear of the car is skidding. *Do not hit the brakes.* Putting on the brakes will only cause the car to skid even more. Turn the steering wheel *gently* to bring the car out of the skid. As you begin to get control again, *gently* accelerate. This will also help to bring the car back under control.

Blowouts

If a tire blows out when you are driving fast, you could lose control. When a rear tire blows out, the car pulls from side to side. If the right front tire blows out, the car pulls to the right. If the left front tire blows out, it pulls to the left.

Tires in good condition should not blow out. Check your tires to make sure they are safe. And always drive with both hands on the steering wheel.

If you have a blowout, get a good hold on the steering wheel. Keep the car in its own lane. Take your foot off the accelerator. *Don't hit the brakes.* Let the engine slow the car. When the car slows to about 20 mph, begin braking. Pull off the road if you can. Stop in a safe place.

Changing a Tire

Never try to change a flat tire in traffic. Keep driving until you can find a safe place. It is better to ruin a tire than to be hit by a car.

Put on your emergency flashers. At night, use flares. Warn other drivers that you are having trouble. To change the tire, follow these steps:

1. Put the car in Park. If you have a standard transmission, put the car in reverse. Then set the parking brake.
2. Put blocks behind the tires to keep the car from rolling.
3. Take off the wheel cover with the jack handle. Loosen the wheel nuts. But don't take them off.

4. Jack up the car until the flat tire is off the ground. Take off the wheel nuts and pull off the tire. (*Never go under a car that is on a jack.*)

5. Put the spare tire on. Put the nuts back on, but do not tighten them all the way. Lower the jack.

6. When all four wheels are on the ground, tighten the nuts. Put the wheel cover back on. Make sure the wheel cover is on tight.

If the Brakes Fail

Have your brakes checked from time to time. This is the best way to keep them in good working condition. But learn what to do if they should fail.

First, pump the brake pedal four or five times. Try to build up enough brake pressure to stop the car. If this does not work, put on the parking brake. The parking brake will slow the car. But it will not last long. Shift to a lower gear. Let the engine bring the car to a stop.

Running off the Road

Some roads have a sharp edge. If your right wheels go over this edge, you could lose control of the car. Watch where you steer. Keep all four wheels on the road at all times. But if you do run off the road, follow these steps:

1. Don't hit the brakes. Take your foot off the accelerator and keep driving straight.

2. Wait until you have slowed before going back on the road. If you try getting back on at high speed, you could skid or roll over.

3. Steer so that your right wheels are about 2 feet off the road. When you have slowed, pull back on the road at a sharp angle.

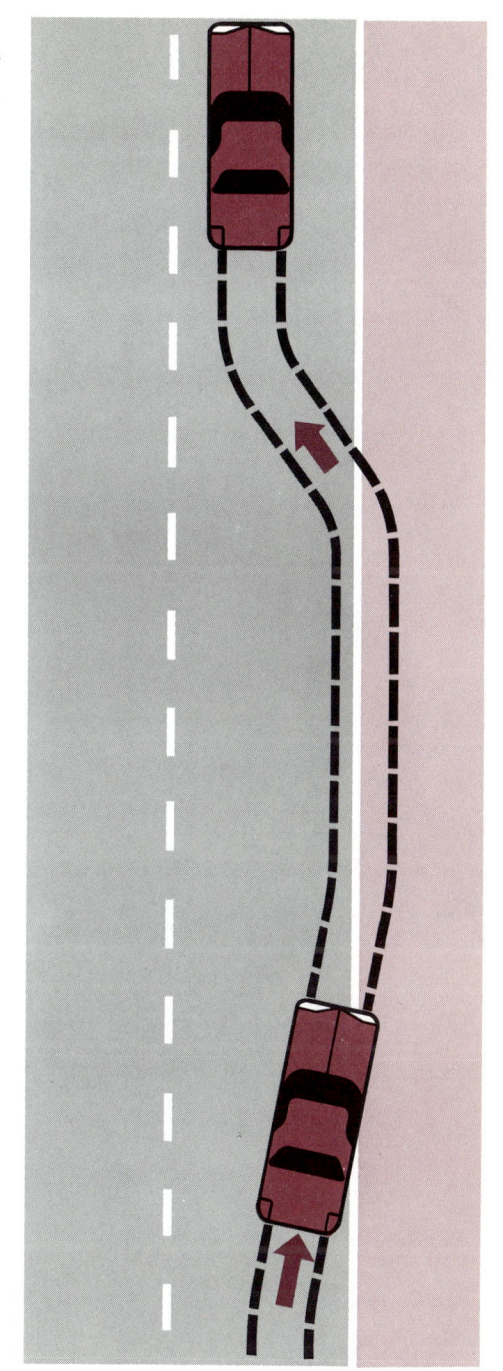

205

Checking What You Have Read

1. The defensive driver thinks ahead. What does this mean? Give examples.
2. The defensive driver always leaves himself an out. Give an example of how a defensive driver might do this.
3. The first rule in defensive driving is to aim high in steering. What does this mean? Give an example.
4. The second rule in defensive driving is to keep your eyes moving. What does this mean? Give an example.
5. The third rule in defensive driving is to get the big picture. What does this mean? Give an example.
6. Why is it dangerous to follow right behind trucks or buses?
7. What does "overdriving headlights" mean? Give an example.
8. When starting on a trip, why should you always try to leave a little early?
9. What are some of the dangers you must watch out for when driving in the country at night?
10. Suppose you are driving at night. What should you do if an oncoming car does not dim its high-beam headlights?
11. The defensive driver can spot trouble-in-the-making. Give two examples of how he does this.
12. When driving through fog, should you use your high beams or low beams? Give a reason for your answer.
13. Suppose you have a blowout. What should you do to keep your car under control? What should you *not* do?

14. Suppose your car begins to skip. What should you do to get it back under control? What should you *not* do?

15. Suppose your right wheels go off the edge of the road. What should you do to get back on the road? What should you *not* do?

To Talk About

1. In your own words, tell what you think defensive driving means. Do others in class agree with you? Do they have anything to add?

2. The defensive driver learns from his mistakes. Think back about driving mistakes you have made. Did you learn anything from these mistakes? Give examples.

3. Suppose your car were to get stuck in snow. Tell how you would go about getting out. What can you do to keep from getting stuck in the first place? What should you carry in your trunk?

4. The defensive driver knows what to do in an emergency. The poor driver does not. He just hopes that nothing bad will ever happen. What is wrong with this kind of thinking?

Things To Do

Look back at the IPDE process on pages 195–197. Come up with ideas of your own for using the IPDE process. Then paint posters to show how you could use the process to become a better defensive driver.

CHAPTER **15**

Planning a Trip

Before you start out on a long trip, plan ahead. Get a road map and plan the route you will take. Most of the time there will be more than one route you can take. One route may be faster than another. But the other route may have more things to see along it. Some of the roads along the way may be better than others. Some mountain passes may be closed in the winter. A road map will help you decide which route is best for you.

Map Reading

On almost all maps north is at the top. South is at the bottom. East is to the right of the map, and west is to the left.

How to read your map of

COLORADO

SCALE OF MILES
0 5 10 20 30 40
ONE INCH EQUALS APPROXIMATELY 18 MILES

HIGHWAY MARKERS
INTERSTATE (25)   UNITED STATES (40)   STATE (56)

ROAD CLASSIFICATIONS
CONTROLLED ACCESS HIGHWAYS — Interchanges
(Entrance and Exit only at Interchanges)
OTHER DIVIDED HIGHWAYS
PRINCIPAL THROUGH HIGHWAYS — Paved
OTHER THROUGH HIGHWAYS — Paved
CONNECTING HIGHWAYS — Paved
LOCAL ROADS In unfamiliar areas inquire locally before using these roads — Paved Gravel Dirt

MILEAGES
MILEAGE BETWEEN TOWNS AND JUNCTIONS 3 4
MILEAGE BETWEEN DOTS 35
LONG DISTANCE MILEAGES SHOWN IN RED

SPECIAL FEATURES
STATE PARKS With Campsites ▲ Without Campsites △
SCHEDULED AIRLINE STOPS ✈
MILITARY AIRPORTS
RECREATION AREAS With Campsites ▲ Without Campsites △
OTHER AIRPORTS
SKI AREAS
MAJOR MTN. ROADS CLOSED IN WINTER — Closed in Winter
SELECTED REST AREAS
TIME ZONE BOUNDARY
POINTS OF INTEREST ■
COUNTY LINES

POPULATION SYMBOLS
⊛ State Capital   ⊗ 2,500 to 5,000   ○ 25,000 to 50,000
○ Under 1,000   ⊙ 5,000 to 10,000   ● 50,000 to 100,000
⊙ 1,000 to 2,500   ● 10,000 to 25,000 ● 100,000 and over

Ⓖ © THE H. M. GOUSHA COMPANY
BOX 6227 • SAN JOSE, CALIF. 95150
A SUBSIDIARY OF THE TIMES MIRROR COMPANY
ALL RIGHTS RESERVED

In one corner of the map is a box showing what the symbols mean. Some of the symbols show the different kinds of roads and highways. Other symbols show how large the towns and cities are. Still other symbols show airports, parks, and railroads. The *scale* of the map is also shown in this box. One inch may equal 10 miles, 20 miles, or more.

On one side of the map is a list of all the towns and cities shown. After each name there is a letter and a number. After Denver, for example, is the letter-number C-9. This letter-number tells you where to find Denver on the map. Look at the letters along the side of the map. Find C. Now look at the numbers along the bottom of the map. Find 9. Bring your finger up from 9 and across from C. There is Denver.

Next to the road symbols on the map are small dots. Between each two dots is a number. The number tells how many miles it is between the dots.

Go over the map carefully before you begin your trip. First, plan your route. Then decide how long it will take to get where you want to go. If your trip will take more than one day, where will you stop? Which town or city will you stay in?

When using freeways, know which exit you want. Mark the exit on the map. Never try to look at your map while driving. If you have a passenger, let him or her look for you. Look at the map yourself only when you have stopped for a rest.

Ready To Go

Before you start, be sure everything is ready. Check your car carefully. Check your headlights, tail lights, and turn signals. Is the engine running well? If not, have the problem fixed before you leave. Are all

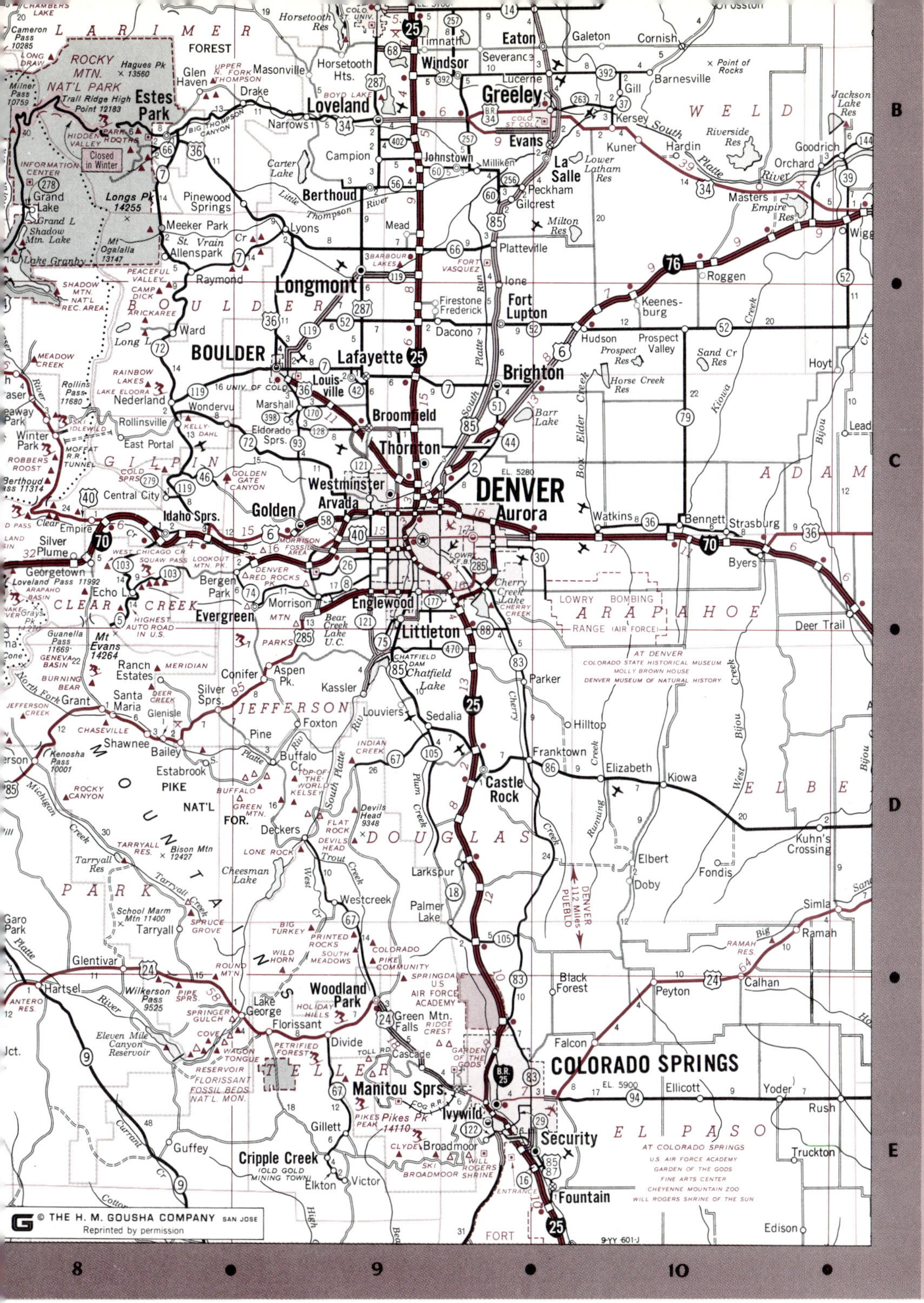

Briggsdale B-10
Brighton • 8,309 . C-9
Bristol F-14
Broadmoor E-9
Broomfield
7,261 . . . . C-9
Brush 3,377 . . . B-11
Buckingham . . . B-11
Buena Vista
1,962 . . . . E-7
Burlington •
2,828 . . . . . . D-13
Cahone G-3
Calhan 465 . . . E-10
Campion B-9
Campo 206 . . . H-13
Canon City •
9,206 . . . . F-9
Carbondale 726 . . D-6
Carlton F-13
Cascade E-9
Castle Rock •
1,531 . . . . D-9
Catherine D-6
Cattle Creek D-6
Cedaredge 581 . . E-5
Center 1,470 . . . G-7
Coaldale F-8
Cokedale 101 . . H-10
Collbran 225 . . . D-4
Colona F-5
Colorado City . . . F-9
Colorado Springs •
135,060 . . . . . E-9
Conejos • H-7
Cope C-12
Cortez • 6,032 . . G-3
Cotopaxi F-8
Cowdrey A-7
Craig • 4,205 . . . B-5
Crawford 171 . . . E-5
Creede • 653 . . . G-6
Crested Butte
372 . . . . E-6
Crestone 34 . . . . F-8
Cripple Creek •
425 . . . . E-9
Crook 199 . . . . A-12
Cross Mountain . . B-4
Crowley 216 . . . F-11
Cuchara H-9
Dacono 360 . . . . C-9
Dailey B-13
De Beque 155 . . . D-4
Deer Trail 574 . C-11
Del Norte •
1,569 . . . . G-7
Delhi G-11
Delta • 3,694 . . . E-4
Denver •
514,678 . . . . . C-9
Devereaux D-5
Devine F-10
Dillon 182 . . . . . C-7
Dinosaur 247 . . . B-3
Divide E-9
Dolores 820 . . . . G-4
Dotsero C-6
Dove Creek •
619 . . . . G-3
Dowd C-7
Doyleville F-7
Drake B-9
Durango •
10,333 . . . . . . H-4
Eads • 795 . . . . E-13
Eagle • 790 . . . . C-6
Eaton 1,389 . . . B-10
Echo Lake C-8
Eckley 193 . . . . C-13
Edwards C-7
Egnar F-3
El Moro H-10
Elbert D-10
Eldorado
Springs C-9
Elizabeth 493 . . D-10
Elk Springs B-4
Elkton E-9
Ellicott E-10
Empire 249 . . . . C-8
Englewood
33,695 . . . . . . C-9
Estes Park
1,616 . . . . B-8
Estrella H-8
Evans 2,570 . . . B-10
Fairplay • 419 . . D-8
Falcon E-10
Firestone 570 . . C-9
Firstview E-13
Flagler 615 . . . D-12
Fleming 349 . . . B-12
Florence 2,846 . . F-9
Florissant E-9
Fort Collins •
43,337 . . . . . . B-9
Fort Garland G-8
Fort Lewis H-4
Fort Lupton
2,489 . . . . C-9
Fort Morgan •
7,594 . . . . . . B-11
Fortification
Hall A-5
Fountain
3,515 . . . . . . E-10
Fowler 1,241 . . F-11
Franktown D-9
Fraser 221 . . . . . C-8
Frederick 696 . . C-9
Fruita 1,822 . . . . D-3
Galatea E-12
Garcia H-8
Gardner G-9
Garfield E-7
Garo Park D-8
Gateview F-6

the tires in good condition? (Be sure to check the spare tire, too.) Are the tires at the right pressure? Is there enough water in the battery? Fill up the gas tank and check the oil. Be sure you have all the tools you may need. Also check your jack. Bring along a spare fan belt and radiator hose.

On Your Way

You should be well rested before you start your trip. Get enough sleep the night before. Then get an early start in the morning. If you live in the city, try to get started before traffic builds up. Give yourself more than enough time to get where you want to go. Then you will have time to meet any problems without feeling that you must hurry.

On the freeway, watch your speed. Check your speedometer every so often. You may find yourself going faster than you think. Keeping your speed down is a good way to save on gas, too.

If you are not sure which road to take, stop and ask directions. Service stations are happy to be of help.

Freeway driving is fast. But it can be tiring. The highway often looks the same mile after mile. Don't drive too long without taking a rest. Stop for a rest after the first three hours. (Or as soon as you begin feeling tired.) After that, stop to rest every 100 miles. You may want to stop more often than this. Always stop when you begin to feel tired.

There are rest areas for your use along most freeways. After you pull in to a rest area, get out and walk around. Get some fresh air. Don't start driving again until you feel rested.

Check your gas gauge from time to time. Your car uses a lot more gas at high speed. Gas stations may be many miles apart. Look for signs telling of service areas. In many service areas you can also get something to eat.

Don't try to drive much more than 500 miles in a day. Stop driving before it gets dark. Even on the freeway, night driving is dangerous and tiring. And you may have trouble finding a motel if you wait too long. Get a good night's sleep. Then you will be ready for another early start in the morning. Check your map again before driving.

Mountain Driving

Your trip may take you into the mountains. The views are beautiful. But keep your eyes on the road! Mountain driving can be dangerous. Often, the roads are not very wide. And there are sharp curves and steep hills. There may also be snow, even in late spring. Listen to the weather reports on your radio. Carry chains if there are reports of snow.

Your car will not have as much power in the mountains. You will need a lot more time and distance to pass. Keep this in mind if you have to pass a slow-moving car or truck. Pass only if it is safe to do so. When going uphill, you may have to shift to a lower gear. You may also need to shift to a lower gear when going down.

Keep an eye on your temperature gauge. Mountain driving can make your engine get too hot. If this happens, pull off the road in a safe place. Be sure to set your parking brake. You may have to add water to your radiator. But don't open the radiator cap while the temperature is high. Wait until the temperature goes down before doing anything. Carry a can of water with you for the radiator.

Add water to the radiator a little at a time, with the engine running. If you add too much water all at once, you could crack the engine block.

Desert Driving

Driving in the desert is not as hard as it once was. Better roads—and better cars—have made desert driving much safer. But there are still dangers to watch for.

Make sure your car is in good condition before driving in the desert. If something breaks, you may have trouble finding help. Towns are few and far between. Check the pressure in your tires before starting. Tires get very hot in the desert. If there is too much pressure in them, you could have a blowout.

Carry a large can of water with you. You may need it if your engine gets too hot. And you may need a drink of water yourself! Also carry a spare fan belt and radiator hose.

Be careful about driving on back roads in the desert. It is easy to get lost. And if you get stuck in the sand, you could be in real trouble. Ask people who live in the area about road conditions before driving on back roads.

Checking What You Have Read

1. Look back at the map on page 211. What is the scale of this map? How many miles does each inch equal?
2. How many miles is it from Colorado Springs to Fountain?
3. What would seem to be the shortest and best route between Boulder and Greeley?
4. Is there an interchange at Deer Trail?
5. What kind of road runs between Franktown and Kuhn's Crossing?
6. What is the number of the highway running through Eaton? Is this an Interstate highway or a U.S. highway?
7. Which town is bigger, Brighton or Fort Lupton? About how many people live in each town?
8. Can you camp at Castlewood Park? (near Castle Rock)
9. Suppose you wanted to go from Estes Park to Grand Lake. What route would you take in August? Would you need a different route in December? Why?

To Talk About

When using freeways, you should know which exit you want. Why is it good planning also to know the exit *before* the one you want?

Things To Do

Get some road maps and plan a long trip. First pick the route you would take. Write down each highway number. Tell why you think this is the best route. How far would you drive each day? Which towns would you stop at for the night? Write a short report about the trip you plan. Also tell how you would get your car ready for this trip.

CHAPTER **16**

Owning a Car

The automobile plays a very big part in American life. There are millions and millions of cars on the road. Many families own two or more cars. Few people could get along very well without their cars. Without automobiles, a lot of people could not get to work. In many cities, there are not enough buses and trains to carry people. Even people who do not like to drive often find themselves having to own automobiles. Before long, you may also want to buy a car. But before you do, be sure you are ready for the responsibility. Buying a car is a big step. Many people do not understand how big a step it is. They are often blinded by their own feelings. All they can think of is having a car. They never think about the responsibility.

Before You Buy

When you own a car, you have a responsibility to yourself and to others. Driving safely is only one part of it (though an important part). Will owning a car make life better for you? Or will the car wind up "owning" you?

It costs a lot of money to own a car—*any* car. Once you buy an automobile, you need money to run it. Here are some of the things you will have to pay for:

- Insurance
- Gas and oil
- Maintenance (tires, tune-ups, filters)
- Repairs
- License plates and registration fees

Depreciation will also cost you money. Depreciation means that each year your car is worth less money. You can never get back all the money you put into a car.

When looking for a used car, get as much information as you can. Take your time, and don't let anyone try to high pressure you. Be sure before you buy.

How much will all this cost you? That depends. Some people have to pay more for insurance than others. Some cars cost more to insure than others. How much gas and oil you use depends on how many miles you drive a year. Maintenance and repair bills are not the same for all drivers. And state fees are different in different states. But owning a car is never cheap. It may cost you from $950 to $1300 *or more* a year to run your car. This is a big responsibility for most people. It is something you should think about before you buy a car of your own.

New Car or Used Car?

Sometimes a new car will not cost much more than some good used cars. If you have enough money, it is better to buy a new car. A new car will not need as many repairs. And if you do have trouble, the new car warranty should protect you. You will not have to pay for parts that are covered by the warranty.

But not everyone has the money to buy a new car. Used cars cost less than new cars. Some are very cheap. But these cheap cars may not be in very good condition. You may have to pay more for repairs than you did for the car. When buying a car, pick the best one you can get for your money.

Picking a Dealer

You don't have to buy a used car from a dealer. Many people sell their automobiles through the newspapers. Or you may know a friend who wants to sell his car. But most of the time, it is better to buy from a dealer. If anything goes wrong with the car, you can take it to the dealer for service.

Most dealers give some kind of warranty on the used cars they sell.

Pick your dealer carefully. Ask your friends if they know of a good used car dealer. Stay away from dealers who offer "no money down" or "$5 down" deals. Watch out for dealers who try to "high pressure" you into buying a car. Some dealers try to make it seem like they are giving cars away. But *no one* gives cars away.

Often the best dealer is one who sells new cars as well as used cars. He takes in many trade-ins. The dealer who sells only used cars often buys cars in poor condition.

Ask the dealer to give you names of others who have bought cars from him. A good dealer will be happy to give you these names. Talk to these people about the dealer. Find out what they have to say about his service.

Picking a Car

Before you pick a dealer, decide what kind of car you want. Do you need a big car? Or would a small car be better for you? How much will the car cost to buy? How much will it cost a year to run? Don't pick a car that you do not have enough money to own. Keep in mind that a car with a big engine uses more gas. It may also cost more to insure.

When you decide what kind of car you want, start looking around. Try one dealer and then another. Look at a lot of different cars. When you find a car that meets your needs, check it over carefully. Here are some of the things you should find out about.

1. If you can, find out who owned the car before. Call the person and ask about the car. Was it ever

in an accident? How many miles did the person drive the car? (Some dealers turn back the odometers. Doing this is against the law. But, still, it is often done.) What problems did he have? Did he follow the owner's manual in having the car serviced?

2. Look over the body and paint in good light. Do you see any new paint? Run your hand over the body. Feel for bumps. New paint over bumps is a sign that the car was in an accident. After body work has been done, the metal is never quite smooth. Also look for rust spots.

3. Check all five tires. Do they have any cuts in them? How much tread is left? Are they all in good condition? Are any of the tires cupped or worn on one side? This is a sign that the front end may be out of line. Or it may mean that the wheels are not balanced.

4. Take hold of one of the front wheels. Shake it from side to side. The tire should not move easily.

Check the front end by shaking a front tire from side to side.

Before taking a test drive, check the steering. You should not have to turn the steering wheel more than 2 inches before the front wheel begins to move.

Listen for noises as you shake the tire. If you hear any banging sounds, something is wrong. The wheel bearings need repair.

5. Push down on one corner of the car. Rock the car up and down a few times. Then stand back and watch. If the car keeps rocking for some time, the shock absorbers are worn out. You would have to buy new ones.

6. Test the doors. Open and close each door a few times. Do the doors open and close easily? When closed, do they fit right? A poor-fitting door is a sign that the car has been in an accident.

7. Check to see if all the windows open and close right. Roll the windows up and down. Do they open and close easily? When closed, do the windows fit right? If not, repair could be expensive.

8. Test the steering. If the car has power steering, you will have to start the engine to test it. If the car does not have power steering, you can test

it without starting the engine. Roll down the window on the driver's side. Stand next to the car so that you can see the left front tire. Gently move the steering wheel from side to side. (Keep the front wheels straight.) How much do you have to turn the wheel before the tire begins to move? There should not be more than 2 inches of free play in the steering. A lot of free play means that the car has had much use.

9. Check the brakes. Push down on the brake pedal with your hand. The pedal should not get closer than 2 inches from the floor. Then press down on the pedal with your foot. Hold the pedal down. If the pedal begins to move toward the floor, something is wrong. Bad brakes are expensive to repair. They are also dangerous.

Test Driving the Car

After you have looked over the car, take it for a test drive. The dealer may want to ride along with you. But be sure that *you* drive. If the dealer will not let you drive the car, go to another dealer. Always test drive a car yourself before buying it.

Some dealers (but not good ones) may ask you to sign a paper before the test drive. Or they may ask you for a "security deposit." *Don't sign anything. Don't give the dealer any money* before a test drive. After the test drive, the dealer might tell you that you have bought the car! Don't be tricked into buying a car you may not want.

Give the car a good road test. Driving around the block will not tell you much. Give the car a chance to warm up. Once it is warm, listen to the engine. Some engines sound all right when cold. But they knock and make noise when warm.

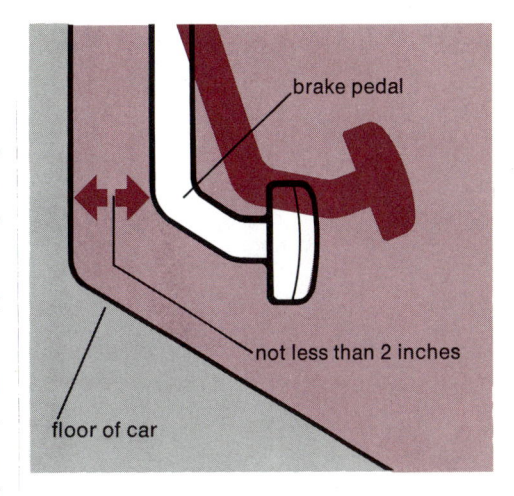

Check all the controls and gauges. Check the lights, turn signals, and horn. Also check the radio, heater, and defroster. Is everything in good working order?

If the car has a standard transmission, check the clutch carefully. Let the clutch out slowly. Note the point where the transmission begins to take hold. The clutch pedal should be no more than 1 to 1½ inches out. At this point the car should begin to move forward.

The car should shift smoothly from gear to gear. It should shift smoothly with a standard or automatic transmission. Listen for any noises as the car shifts. Noises in the transmission mean expensive trouble.

Test the steering by making a few sharp right and left turns. Is the car easy to control as you turn? Is there a lot of free play in the steering wheel?

Drive the car down a flat road. Take your hands off the wheel. Does the car pull to one side? If it does, the front end may be out of line. Or the frame may be bent.

Find a road where there is not much traffic and test the brakes. Stop the car five or six times from 45 mph. Push down harder on the brake each time. Does the car stop easily each time? Or does it take longer and longer to stop? Does the car pull to one side when you put on the brakes? Do the brakes make noise?

As you drive, get the feel of the car. How does it ride? Does the ride seem too soft or too hard? These could be signs of trouble. Do the front wheels begin to shake when you get to a certain speed? Drive the car over a rough road. Does the car make a lot of noise as it goes over the bumps? Is it hard to control? If so, don't buy the car. Repair would be expensive.

Other Tests

If you can, have a friend follow you in another car. Have him watch how the car drives. Do any of the wheels seem to shake? Do the rear wheels follow behind the front wheels? Or do they follow a little to one side? If they do, the car has a bent frame. Don't buy it.

Have your friend watch for smoke from the tail pipe. If he sees puffs of blue smoke when you shift, the car needs new rings. If it smokes all the time, the engine needs a lot of work. You would be better off looking at another car.

After the test drive, check under the car for leaks. Look for drops of oil and water. Also check the muffler for leaks. But be careful—the muffler will be hot!

When test driving a used car, watch for smoke. Heavy smoke from the exhaust is always a bad sign.

Take another good look at the car. Check things over again. If you spotted any problems on the test drive, look into them. How much would these problems cost to repair?

While the engine is still warm (but not hot!) take off the radiator cap. Start the engine. Look into the radiator. Watch for bubbles coming up, or for oil. Oil or bubbles mean there is a leak somewhere. Repair could be expensive.

Making Sure

The more you know about cars, the better your chances are of getting a good one. But most people don't know that much about cars. To be sure the used car you want is a good one, get some help. If you know a good mechanic, ask him to check the car for you. (Don't ask one of the dealer's mechanics to help you.) You will have to pay the mechanic. But it will be money well spent.

Or you may be able to take the car to a diagnostic test center. There may be a diagnostic test center near your home. These centers have equipment that many mechanics do not have. The tests will cost $20 to $35. But, again, it will be money well spent. After the tests, you will know if the car is in good condition or not.

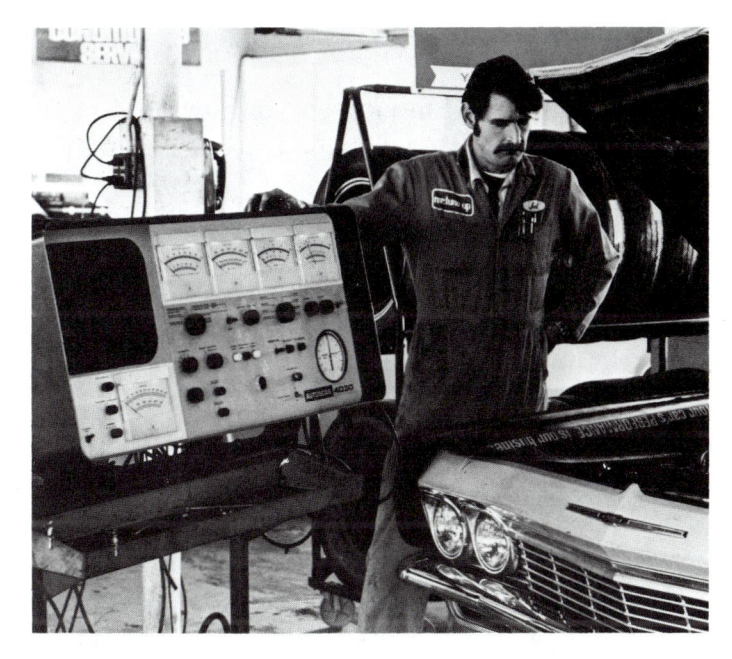

Paying for the Car

Before you buy a car, decide how you will pay for it. Some people pay cash-in-full. But most people buy their cars "on time." They make a down payment. And they borrow the rest of the money to pay for the car. They pay a part of this money back each month until the loan is paid. When a person borrows money, he must pay for the use of the money. The longer it takes him to pay back the money, the more it costs him.

When you buy a car, you should pay one-third or more down. If the car costs $900, you should make a $300 down payment. Never borrow money to make a down payment. If you don't have enough for a one-third down payment, look for a cheaper car. Stay away from dealers who offer "no money down" deals. You will end up paying much more for the car in the long run.

Borrowing Money

You can not borrow money on your own until you are legally of age. But what you learn now can save you money in years to come.

There are many places where you can borrow money. Banks, loan companies, and car dealers all make loans. They do not all charge the same. Interest rates are different at different places. They are also different in different states. The interest rate on a car may be from 6 percent to 12 percent or more. Some loan companies charge up to 24 percent a year for a loan.

What does all this mean? Suppose you want to borrow $600 for one year. If the interest rate is 6 percent, the loan will cost you $36. For the use of $600, you must pay back $636. If the interest rate is 18 percent, you must pay back $708. At 24 percent, you would have to pay back $744.

Most of the time, you can get the best interest rate from a bank. Loan companies charge more. Some car dealers may charge even more. Shop around before you decide. Get the best deal you can. Interest rates are not always easy to understand. Always ask how much the loan will cost *in dollars*. The bank or loan company may want you to take out insurance on the loan. This insurance protects the lender if anything should happen to you. The cost of the insurance should also be counted as part of the loan cost.

You can get a loan for 6, 12, 18, 24 or even 36 months. The longer you take the loan for, the more it will cost. If you can, take the loan for not longer than 18 months. The sooner you pay off the loan, the sooner the car will be yours.

Legal Agreements

If you pay cash for a car, you sign a *bill of sale*. The dealer also signs it. In most states, the bill of sale is then sent to the Department of Motor Vehicles. The Department of Motor Vehicles sends the owner the title for the car. The *title* shows that you are the legal owner.

If you buy a car on time, you sign a *sales contract*. This contract is a legal agreement. Once you sign it, the law says you must follow it. Read the sales contract carefully. It is best to have someone with you. Have this person also read the contract before you sign it.

Make sure that all of these things are written in the contract:

- the price of the car and the price of any accessories (radio, heater, and so on)
- the down payment you made
- the unpaid balance (how much you still must pay)
- any other charges (taxes, registration fees)
- the number of monthly payments and the size of each payment

Make sure all the blanks in the contract are filled in or crossed out. If there are blanks, don't sign. Other charges could be written in after you sign.

Until you make all the payments, you are not the legal owner. The bank or the car dealer is the legal owner. The legal owner will hold the title. But the car will be registered in your name.

With your license plates, you will get a *certificate of registration.* The certificate of registration shows that you are the registered owner. Keep this certificate of registration in your car.

When you make all the payments, the legal owner will turn over the title to you. The title shows that you are now the legal owner of the car. Keep the title in a safe place (*not* in the car). You will need it when you sell the car.

Taking Care of Your Car

Some cars still look new when they are six or seven years old. Other cars look old after just one year. This is because some drivers take care of their cars and others don't. But how a car *looks* is only one part of the story. If a person does not take care of his car, it will not keep running well. He will have to pay a lot more for repairs. And his car will not be worth much when he sells it.

Your first car may not be a new one. But if you keep it in good condition, you can drive it a long time. Follow the owner's manual. The owner's manual will tell you how often the car should be serviced. It will tell you what should be done to keep the car running well.

How you drive also matters. If you drive hard, the car will soon wear out. If you drive in a responsible way, the car should last for years.

For longer and more even wear, tires should be rotated every 5,000 miles.

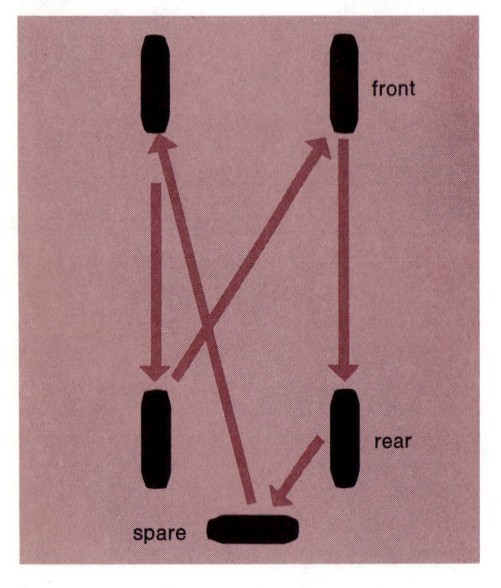

The Road Ahead

You have now learned the basic skills of driving. But you still have much to learn. Getting your driver's license is just the first step. As the years go by, try to become the best driver in town.

- Aim for smooth starts, smooth stops, and smooth turns. The smooth driver makes driving look easy. But he knows that safe, smooth driving is not easy. It takes real skill. And his passengers know it, too. They know that the smooth driver is a person who knows what he is doing.
- Don't let anyone talk you into doing something you know is foolish. A car is not a toy. And a highway is not a race track.
- Keep learning. Traffic laws change. Traffic conditions change. Cars change. Keep up with the changes.
- Take time. Take time to keep your car in good condition. Take time to think ahead. Take time to get where you are going.

How well and how much you learn is up to you. From now on, you are in the driver's seat.

Checking What You Have Read

1. About how much a year does it cost to own and run an automobile?
2. What is depreciation? How does depreciation add to the cost of owning an automobile?
3. How can you tell if a used car has been in an accident? Name two things you should look for.
4. When buying a car, how much of a down payment should you make?
5. What is a certificate of registration?
6. Why is it important to keep the title to your car in a safe place?

To Talk About

1. Most people want to own their own cars. But sometimes a person buys a car without thinking about the responsibility of owning it. The car winds up "owning" the owner. Do you know of any examples of this? What happened?
2. Why is it best to stay away from dealers who offer "no money down" deals?
3. Suppose you want to buy a car, but you don't know much about cars. What can you do to make sure the car you buy is a good one? Who can you ask for help?

Things To Do

Keep a record of how much it costs to run your family car. Keep this record for two months. How much did gasoline and oil cost? Were any repairs needed? Parking fees, car washes, and traffic fines should also be listed. These, too, are a part of the cost of owning a car. Also work out how much insurance costs for the two months. Then write a short report about the cost of owning a car. Keep in mind that depreciation adds to this cost.

Index

Index

A

Acceleration, 203, 205
Acceleration lane, 179–180
Accelerator, 108, 109, 122, 171
Accidents, 195
   in city, 149
   on country highways, 169, 171
   cutting down on, 11–12
   and defensive driving, 32–34, 49, 147, 158, 171, 173, 180–181, 191, 195, 196, 199
   and force of impact, 47–48
   on freeways, 177, 180
   helping people injured in, 78, 79
   and insurance, 80–83, 84
   laws about, 78, 80
   motorcycle riders in, 187, 188, 189, 190, 191, 192
   number each year, 11
   and pedestrians, 48, 157, 158, 161–163
   rear-end, 150, 176, 180
   reports of, 78, 80
   and seat belts, 48, 105
   and tailgating, 51, 147, 150, 171, 180, 191, 198
Air filter, 90–91
Alcohol
   and accidents, 22
   how it changes people, 22–23
   and pedestrians, 160
Alley turn, 133
"Almost" stopping, 151
Alternator, 91, 102, 104
Alternator warning light, 102–103, 104
Angle parking, 136–137
Arm signals. *See* Turn signals, hand
Automatic transmission car, 94, 116–120
   angle parking, 136–137
   backing, 131
   gear positions, 94, 110, 116
   getting under way, 118
   parallel parking, 138–139
   parking on hill, 140–141
   starting engine, 117
   starting on hill, 141
   stopping, 120
Automatic transmission selector, 110, 116
Automobile maintenance, 178, 210, 212, 214, 230
   air filter, 90–91
   alternator and battery, 103, 104
   brakes, 149, 205
   engine, 22, 90–91, 97, 98, 104
   lights, 162, 201
   lubrication, 97, 98
   oil change, 102

Automobile maintenance *(continued)*
  radiator, 98, 104
  steering system, 134
  tires, 136, 203 (illus. 178)
Automobiles
  buying new, 219
  buying used, 219–227
  cost of owning, 218–219
  dealers, 219–220, 227, 228
  depreciation, 218
  driving controls, 108–110
  gauges, 103–104
  indicators, 101–104
  insurance, 80–84
  legal agreements, 229–230
  payments, 227–229
  safety controls, 105–108
  systems, 90–98
  See also Automobile maintenance
Axle, 94

B
Backing, 109, 131–132
  from angle parking space, 137
  with automatic transmission, 131
  dangers of, 131, 137
  on freeway, 183
  to parallel park, 138
  with standard transmission, 132
Back roads, 214
Back-up lights, 106
Bad weather, 199, 201–202
  and motorcycle riding, 190
  and pedestrians, 163
  See also Road conditions; Safe speed for conditions
Banked curve, 45
Battery, 91, 102, 104, 178
"Beating" traffic lights, 149
Bill of sale, 229
Blinding headlights, 16–17, 201 (illus. 31)

Blind spot, 180, 181, 191 (illus. 181)
Blowouts, 203–204
  front tire, 203
  rear tire, 203
Bodily injury liability insurance, 81–82
Borrowing money, 228–229
  See also Buying a car
Brake drum, 96
Brake lights, 106, 181
Brake pedal, 96, 109
Brakes, 46, 120, 172
  condition of, 178, 223, 224
  and friction, 41–42
  what to do if they fail, 205
  worn, 42, 50
Brake shoes, 96
Braking
  in blowout, 204
  and friction, 96
  on hills, 46, 171–172
  when running off road, 205
  in skids, 203
Braking distance, 46, 49, 50 (table 50)
  See also Braking time; Following distance; Stopping distance; Tailgating
Braking system, 96
Braking time, 42, 49, 50
  See also Braking distance; Following distance; Stopping distance; Tailgating
Breakdowns, 182
Buses, 150, 153, 165, 171
Buying a car
  borrowing money, 228–229
  checking with mechanic, 226–227
  cost of owning, 218–219
  dealers, 219–220, 227, 228
  deciding what kind, 220

legal agreements, 229–230
new, 219
payments, 227–228
responsibility of owning, 217–218
used (*see* Buying a used car, what to check; Road test, what to check)
Buying a used car, what to check (illus. 221, 222, 223)
    body and paint, 221
    brakes, 223
    doors, 222
    front wheels, 221–222
    for leaks, 225–226
    if it has been in accident, 220–221, 222
    radiator, 226
    shock absorbers, 222
    steering, 222–223
    tires, 221
    windows, 222
    See also Road test, what to check
Buying insurance. *See* Insurance, automobile

C

Carbon monoxide, 21–22, 107
Carburetor, 90
Car trouble. *See* Automobile maintenance
Centrifugal force (illus. 43)
    and curves, 44–45
    and friction, 43–44
    and speed, 44
Certificate of registration, 230
Chains, 202, 213
Changing lanes, 147–148
    on freeway, 181, 182, 183
Children, 131, 158, 160, 199
Clutch, 92–93, 224 (illus. 93)
    changing gears, 110
    starting engine, 122
    stopping, 123
    See also Clutch pedal
Clutch pedal, 93, 94, 110
Collision. *See* Accidents
Collision insurance, 82
Color blind drivers, 18
Comprehensive insurance, 83
Controls
    for driving, 108–111
    for safety, 105–108
    See also Gauges; Indicators
Coolant, 98
Cooling system, 98
Crankshaft, 92
"Creeping," 120
Crosswalks, 58, 63, 128, 133, 150, 151, 165 (illus. 150)
Crowned curve, 45
Curves, 44–45, 172, 203 (illus. 45)

D

Dealer. *See* Buying a car, dealers
Deceleration lane, 183
Defensive driving, 32–34, 49, 147, 158, 171, 173, 180–181, 191, 195–205 (illus. 171, 172, 173, 198)
Defroster, 107, 201
Department of Motor Vehicles, 13, 57, 78, 229
Depreciation, 218
Desert driving, 214
Diagnostic test center, 227
Differential, 94
Dimmer switch, 105–106
Dimming lights, 105, 106, 201
Dipstick, 97, 103
Distributor, 91
DO NOT PASS signs, 174
Driver education, 11–12, 84
Driver, physical condition of, 12–24

Driver responsibility, 231
  in accidents, 78–80
  to buy insurance, 80–82
Driver's license, 12–13, 34, 57, 231
Driver who is always right, 31
Driveshaft, 94
Driving personalities, 28–32, 146
Driving when tired or sleepy, 20–21, 212–213
Down payment, 227–228

E
Electrical system, 91
Emergencies, 203–205
Emergency flashers, 108, 182, 204
Emergency vehicles, 58, 78
Engine, 90–91
  as brake, 46, 123, 204, 205
  condition, 178
  See also Automobile maintenance, engine
Exhaust system, 22
Eye problems, 13–14
Eyes, testing, 13–15 (illus. 15)

F
Fan, 98, 104
Fan belt, 104, 178, 214
Farm vehicles, 171
First gear (standard transmission), 93–94, 121, 122, 123
Flares, 79, 182, 204
Flat curve, 45
Flat tire, how to change, 204–205
Flywheel, 92–93
Fog, 202
Following distance, 18, 51–52, 147, 171 (illus. 51)
  behind motorcycle, 191
  when beginning to pass, 176
  See also Braking distance; Braking time; Stopping distance; Tailgating

Force of impact. *See* Impact
Four-way stops, 152
Freeway driving, 177–183
  accidents, 177, 180, 181, 183
  condition of car, 178
  defensive driving, 180–181
  emergencies, 182
  following distance, 180
  getting off, 178, 179, 182–183, 210 (illus. 183)
  getting on, 179–180 (illus. 179)
  interchanges, 177, 178, 179, 182–183 (illus. 183)
  judging entrance, 179
  median strip, 177
  passing, 181
  planning ahead, 178, 182
  rearview mirrors, use of, 180, 181
  safety of, 177
  signs, 179, 182
  speed, 177, 178, 179, 180, 181, 182, 183, 212, 213
Friction, 41 (illus. 41, 42)
  in braking, 41–42
  and centrifugal force, 43
  engine, 97
  in mud, snow, ice, 41
  between tires and road, 41, 42
  and turning, 43
Friction point, 122, 132, 142, 224 (illus. 122)
Fuel filter, 90
Fuel gauge, 104
Fuel pump, 90
Fuel system, 90–91
Full stop, 61, 134, 151

G
Gasoline gauge, 104, 213
Gauges
  fuel, 104, 213
  temperature, 103–104

See also Controls for driving;
 Controls for safety; Indicators
Gears. *See* Automatic transmission
 selector; First gear; Low gear;
 Neutral gear; Park gear;
 Reverse gear; Second gear;
 Third gear
Gearshift lever, 110, 121
 See also Shifting
Getting under way (illus. 119)
 automatic transmission, 118
 standard transmission, 122–123
Good driving, 12, 32–34, 52, 57,
 135, 149, 195–199
Gravity, 45 (illus. 46)
 and driving on hills, 46
 and stopping distance, 46

H
Hand-over-hand steering, 127–128
Hand signals. *See* Turn signals,
 hand
Headlights, 12, 105–106, 161, 162,
 201, 210, 224
 being blinded by, 16–17, 31
 flashing at pedestrians, 198
 flashing when passing, 176
 in fog and rain, 202
 motorcycle, 189, 191
 overdriving, 200
Hearing and driving, 18–19, 159,
 173 (illus. 19)
Heater, 107
High-beam headlights. *See*
 Headlights
High gear, 94
 See also Third gear
Hills, 121, 171–172
 braking distance on, 46
 lower gear use on, 46
 on two-lane roads, 171
Hood, 182
Horn, 107, 137, 159, 162, 176, 198

Hot head, 30

I
Ice. *See* Snow
Ignition key, 108–109, 117, 120
Ignition switch, 108–109
Impact, 47–48 (chart 47)
 and "give," 48
 and speed, 47
 and weight, 48
Indicators
 alternator warning light,
  102–103, 104
 high-beam headlights, 106
 odometer, 102
 oil pressure warning light, 103, 104
 parking brake, 109
 speedometer, 101–102
 turn signals, 107–108
 See also Controls for driving;
 Controls for safety; Gauges
Information signs, 62 (illus. 70)
 See also Road markings; Road
 signs; Traffic signals
Insurance, automobile, 80–84, 220
 how it works, 80–81
 kinds of, 81–84
 and state laws, 82
Interchanges, 177, 178, 179, 182–
 183 (illus. 183)
Interest rates, 228–229
Intersections, 149–153
 "blind," 153
 dangers of, 148, 172–173
 flashing lights at, 60
 making U-turn at, 133
 right-of-way at, 58
 traffic signals at, 60
 uncontrolled, 153
IPDE process, 195–197

J
Jack, automobile, 204, 205

Judgment
  of distance, 17–18, 152, 174
  of following distance, 51
  when getting on freeway, 179
  when passing, 174
  of safe speed for conditions (*see* Safe speed for conditions)
  of speed, 17–18, 152, 161, 174

K
Keeping up with traffic, 30, 146, 170, 180, 183 (illus. 30)

L
Lanes (illus. 147)
  acceleration, 179–180
  deceleration, 183
  left, 147, 181
  right, 147, 148, 181
Learning from mistakes, 32, 33, 187, 196
Learning to drive
  backing, 131–132
  getting under way, 118, 122–123, 141, 142
  operating controls, 105–111, 116, 121, 123
  parking, 135–141
  passing, 175–176 (illus. 174, 175)
  starting, 117, 122
  steering, 118, 127–128
  stopping, 120, 123
  turning, 128–130
  turning around, 132–135
Leaving the car, 120, 163–164 (illus. 164)
Left turn, 18, 62–63, 128–130 (illus. 130)
  ending position, 128
  position of front wheels, 128
  starting position, 130
Light controls, 105–106
Lines. *See* Road markings

Loans
  cost of, 228–229
  length of, 229
Locks, door, 115
Low-beam headlights. *See* Headlights
Low gear, in mud or sand, 116
Lubricating system, 97

M
Map reading, 178, 182, 209–210 (illus. 210, 211)
Map scale, 210
Map symbols, 210
Median strip, 177
Medical costs insurance, 83
Medicines and drugs, 23
Minimum speed limit, 180
Motorcycles
  accidents, 187, 188, 189, 190, 191, 192
  bad weather, 190
  building riding skills, 188
  following distance, 191
  maintenance, 189
  passing, 191
  protection for rider, 189
  rules for safe riding, 191–192
  watching out for, 190–191
  skids, 189–190
  stopping distance, 191
Mountain driving, 213–214

N
Nature's traffic laws, 41–52
  centrifugal force, 43–45
  force of impact, 47–48
  friction, 41–42
  gravity, 45–46
  stopping distance, 48–52
Nervous driver, 30
Neutral gear, 121, 122, 123
Night driving, 200–201

dangers of, 16
headlight use in, 17
and pedestrians, 16, 161–162
No passing areas, 174–175

O

Odometer, 102
Oil, 97
Oil dipstick, 97, 103
Oil filter, 97, 104
Oil hose, 104
Oil pan, 97, 104
Oil pressure warning light, 103, 104
Oil pump, 97, 103, 104
One-way streets, 148
Overdriving headlights, 200
Owner, legal, 229, 230
Owning a car
   cost of, 218–219
   responsibility of, 217–218

P

Painted lines. *See* Road markings
Parallel parking, 138–139
   distance from curb, 138
   getting out of space, 139
   position before backing, 138
   size of space, 138
Park gear, 110, 116, 117, 120, 136, 138, 140–141, 204
Parking brake, use of, 109, 120
   if brakes fail, 205
   when starting engine, 117, 122
   when starting on hill, 141, 142
Parking lights, 105, 106
Parking lots, 136, 137
Parking uphill and downhill, 140–141
   with curb, 140
   without curb, 141
   gears, 140, 141
   wheel positions, 140–141

Passengers, 33, 48, 83, 105, 115, 189, 195, 210
Passing, 18, 174–176 (illus. 174, 175)
   across broken lines, 62–63
   dangers in, 174–175
   on freeways, 181
   judgment, 174
   motorcycles, 191
   on mountain roads, 213–214
   across solid lines, 63
   speed, 174
Paying for a car. *See* Buying a car
Pedestrians
   and alcohol, 160
   in bad weather, 163
   crossing in middle of block, 158
   and drugs, 160
   on left side of road, 165
   at night, 161–162, 201
   old people as, 159–160
   right-of-way of, 58, 128, 151, 165
   safety rules for, 165
   seeing and being seen by, 159, 161–163, 165, 198
Physical condition, changing, 23–24
Physical problems and driving, 13–19
Planning ahead, 178, 182, 209, 210, 213
   See also Defensive driving
Police, 31–32, 57, 58, 78–79, 149, 182
Power brakes, 109
Power steering, 109, 118, 222–223
Power train, 92–94 (illus. 92)
Property damage liability insurance, 82
Pulling off to side of road, 21, 182, 202, 213

R

Radiator, 98, 104, 178, 214, 224

Radiator hose, 104, 214
Railroad crossings, 173 (illus. 68, 173)
  and motorcycles, 192
Railroad crossing signs, 62, 173 (illus. 62, 68)
Reaction distance, 49, 171 (table 50)
  See also Braking distance; Braking time; Reaction time; Safe speed for conditions; Stopping distance; Tailgating
Reaction time, 49, 50
  See also Braking distance; Braking time; Reaction distance; Safe speed for conditions; Stopping distance; Tailgating
Rearview mirrors, use of, 105, 115, 189, 199 (illus. 106)
  and blind spot, 180, 181, 191
  in freeway driving, 180, 181
  in getting under way, 118, 122
  inside, 115, 171, 176
  outside, 115, 164
  when passing, 175, 176
  when stopping, 120, 123
Red light, flashing, 58, 60 (illus. 65)
Regulatory signs, 62 (illus. 69, 70)
  See also Road markings; Road signs; Traffic signals
Rest areas, 213
Reverse gear, 94, 121
Right-of-way rules (illus. 59)
  car going straight, 58
  car on right, 58
  emergency vehicles, 58
  four-way stop, 152
  green light, 60
  intersection, 58
  making left turn, 63
  oncoming car, 152
  pedestrian in crosswalk, 58
  slow driver, 33
  through street, 58
  two-way stop, 151
  uncontrolled intersection, 153
  yield sign, 62
Right turn, 64, 128–129 (illus. 129)
Road conditions, 51, 147, 163, 200, 214
  and friction, 41–42, 44
  and rain, 44, 50, 202
  and skidding, 42, 190, 199, 201, 203
  and snow, 202, 203, 213
  and speed, 42, 169–170, 171, 172
Road hog, 31
Road markings, 201 (illus. 63, 71)
  arrows, 64, 148
  broken white lines, 62–63
  crosswalk lines, 63
  solid double center lines, 63, 133, 174
  solid single lines, 63, 174
  stop lines, 64
  See also Road signs; Traffic signals
Road signs (illus. 61, 65–70, 72)
  DO NOT PASS, 174, 175
  entrance to freeway, 182
  exit from freeway, 179
  information, 44, 179, 182, 213
  one-way, 148
  railroad crossing, 61–62, 173
  regulatory, 44, 69, 70
  speed limit, 44, 61, 146–147, 149, 170, 172, 180, 183
  stop, 20, 61–62, 151, 152
  U-turn, 133
  warning, 61–62
  yield, 44, 62
  See also Road markings; Traffic signals
Roads, miles of paved in U.S., 11
Road test, what to check, 223–225

brakes, 224
controls and gauges, 224
"feel," 224
frame, 225
smoke from tailpipe, 225
steering, 224
transmission, 224
"Rocking" out of snow, 202
Rolling over, 205
Rules
   for pedestrians, 165
   for safe driving, 18, 23, 32, 48, 198, 199 (*see also* Defensive driving)
   for safe motorcycle riding, 191–192
Rules of the road, 12, 57–64 (illus. 59)
Running off the road, 22, 205
"Running the red light," 60

S

Safe speed for conditions, 42, 44, 147, 169–170, 172, 196, 200
   See also Road conditions; Speed; Speed limit
Sales contract, 229–230
Sand, 202
Seat belts, 48, 105, 115 (illus. 48, 105)
Seat lever, 105, 115
Second gear, 94, 121, 122, 123
"Security deposit," 223
Seeing and driving, 14, 20
   and hearing, 19
   motorcycles, 190–191
   at night, 16–17
   to sides, 14–15 (illus. 15)
   See also Pedestrians
Service areas, 213
Shifting, 121 (illus. 111)
   down, 123, 172, 205, 214
   in getting under way, 122–123
   when parking, 136, 138–141
   in snow, 202
   when starting on hill, 141–142
   when stopping, 123
   when turning, 128
   to back up, 131–132
Show-off, 29
Signals
   hand and electrical (illus. 58)
   to slow or stop, 138, 149, 151, 181 (*see also* Stopping)
   traffic police, 149 (*see also* Traffic signals)
   turn (*see* Turn signals)
Skidding, 189–190, 199, 203, 205 (illus. 203)
Slowing down
   in bad weather, 147, 170, 203
   on curves, 44, 45, 172
   in deceleration lane, 183
   in emergencies, 204, 205
   on hills, 46, 171–172
   at intersections, 60, 148, 149, 151, 153, 162, 172–173
   on motorcycle, 190–191
   at night, 16, 17, 147, 162, 170, 200
   at railroad crossings, 173
   to stop, 120, 123
   when not feeling well, 20
   when there are pedestrians, 163
   when turning, 123, 128, 129, 130
   where children are playing, 158, 160, 199
   at yield sign, 62
Smooth driving, 231
Snow, 41–42, 202, 203, 213
Spark plugs, 91
Speed
   in acceleration lane, 179
   and accidents, 47–48, 51, 105, 147, 169–170, 171, 177, 180–181, 188, 190

Speed *(continued)*
  in bad weather, 147, 170, 190, 203
  on curves, 45, 203
  on freeway, 177, 178, 212, 213
  on hills, 46, 171–172
  at intersections, 162
  leaving freeway, 183
  at night, 147
  and pedestrians, 162
  near schools and parks, 160
  and shifting, 121, 122, 123, 128, 172
  in traffic, 29, 146–147
  when crossing railroad tracks, 173
  when passing, 176
  See also Safe speed for conditions; Slowing down; Speed limit
Speed limit, 101–102, 146, 147, 170, 180, 181
  See also Safe speed for conditions; Slowing down; Speed
Speedometer, 101–102, 183, 212
Standard gearshift selector, 110, 121
Standard transmission car, 121–123
  angle parking, 136–137
  backing, 132
  gear positions, 92–94, 110, 121, 123 (illus. 93)
  getting under way, 122–123
  parallel parking, 138
  parking on hill, 140–141
  starting engine, 110, 122
  starting on hill, 141–142
  stopping, 123
Starting the engine, 108–109, 117, 122, 141–142 (illus. 117)
State laws, 57, 64, 79
  and motorcycle riding, 189, 191, 192

Steering, 203, 205, 224
  in backing, 131, 137
  hand-over-hand, 127–128
  "10 and 2" position, 118
Steering column, 95
Steering system, 95
Steering wheel, 109, 223
Stop lights. *See* Traffic signals
Stopping
  in acceleration lane, 180
  in crosswalk, 150
  at intersection, 149–150
  position behind other car, 150
  standard transmission car, 123
  See also Signalling to stop
Stopping distance, 42, 48–51, 169–170, 171, 196, 200 (table 50)
  in bad weather, 163, 201
  and gravity, 46
  with power brakes, 109
  and reaction distance, 49
  See also Braking distance; Following distance; Reaction time; Tailgating
Stop signs, 20, 61–62, 151, 152 (illus. 65)
Sun visors, 107

T
Tailgating, 51, 147, 150, 171, 180, 191, 198
Tail lights, 106
Temperature gauge, 103, 214
"10 and 2" steering position, 118, 127–128 (illus. 118)
Third gear, 121, 123
Thoughtless driver, 31
Three-point turn (Y-turn), 134–135 (illus. 135)
Tire rotation (illus. 230)
Tires, 42, 44, 178, 214, 221
  worn, 42, 44, 50, 203
Title, 229, 230

Traffic lanes, 147–148, 177, 179–180, 181, 183
Traffic lights. *See* Traffic signals
Traffic policemen, 149
Traffic signals, 148–149, 151, 196 (illus. 65)
  arrows, 60
  flashing lights, 60, 62, 173
  how often they change, 148
  meaning of colors, 18
  for pedestrian crossing, 151, 165
  position of colors, 18, 60
  set for posted speed, 149
Transmission, 93–94, 224
  See also Automatic transmission car; Standard transmission car
Trips
  car maintenance, 210, 212
  desert driving, 214
  map reading, 209–210, 213
  mountain driving, 213–214
  night driving, 213
  picking route, 209–210
Trouble-in-the-making, 34, 49, 89, 181, 196, 199 (illus. 35, 197)
  See also Defensive driving
Turning
  across lines, 62–63
  hand-over-hand steering, 127–128
  and pedestrians, 151
  speed, 128
  standard transmission car, 128
  timing, 128
  See also Left turn; Right turn
Turning around
  around-the-block turn, 132
  intersection turn, 133
  three-point turn (Y-turn), 133, 134–135
  U-turn, 133–134
Turn signals, 58, 107–108 (illus. 34, 58)

changing lanes, 176, 179, 181, 182, 183
getting under way, 118, 122, 141, 142
hand, 58, 118, 122
left, 107, 129, 130, 134, 135, 139, 176, 179
parking, 136, 138, 139
right, 107, 128, 136
Two-Second Rule, 51–52, 180 (illus. 51)
  See also Following distance
Two-way stops, 151

U
Uninsured motorist insurance, 82
Used car dealers, 219–220, 227, 228
Used cars, 219–228
U-turn, 132, 133–134 (illus. 134)

V
Vehicle code book, 57, 64

W
WALK signal, 151, 165
Warning signs, 61 (illus. 66–68)
  See also Road markings; Road signs; Traffic signals
Warranty, 219, 220
Water pump, 98, 104
Windshield, 16, 48, 107, 162, 199, 201
Windshield washers, 106
Windshield wipers, 106, 201

XYZ
X-shaped railroad signs, 62, 173
Yellow light, flashing, 60
Yielding right-of-way, 196, 198
  See also Right-of-way rules
Yield sign, 44, 62 (illus. 66)
Y-turn, 134–135

Photo Credits

AC Transit, Oakland, California, 146; Aetna Life & Casualty, Hartford, Connecticut, 33 (right), 198; American Safety Equipment Corporation, Encino, California, 48; BMW/Butler & Smith, Inc., Norwood, New Jersey, 188; Chet Born, San Francisco Fire Department, San Francisco, California, 19 (upper left); California Department of Motor Vehicles, Sacramento, California, 13, 79; California Division of Highways, Sacramento, California, 21, 180; Chevrolet Motor Division, General Motors Corporation, Detroit, Michigan, 102; Chrysler Corporation, Detroit, Michigan, 89; Educational Affairs Department, Ford Motor Company, Dearborn, Michigan, 10; Federal Highway Administration, Washington, D.C., 73 (center left), 213; Humble Oil & Refining Company, Houston, Texas, 212; Dick Kharibian, 22, 71 (lower right), 73 (top), 78, 158 (left), 214, 226; Nick Pavloff, 30, 32 (left), 33 (right), 56 (center), 57 (right), 66 (bottom), 73 (bottom left), (center right), 83, 123, 137, 148, 152, 160, 165, 178, 182, 189, 197, 222, 225, 226, 231; Jerry J. Puff, 102, 103, 108, 109, 159 (left), 190, 201, 221, 222 (top); San Francisco Department of Public Works, Division of Traffic Engineering, San Francisco, California, 11, 60, 73 (center right); *The San Mateo Times*, San Mateo, California, 20, 170; Santa Fe Railway, 19 (lower left); Texas Highway Department, Austin, Texas, 14; UPI-Compix., 163; Vermont Department of Highways, Montpelier, Vermont, 40, 44, 63, 73 (lower right), 177. All other photographs by T. Belina.